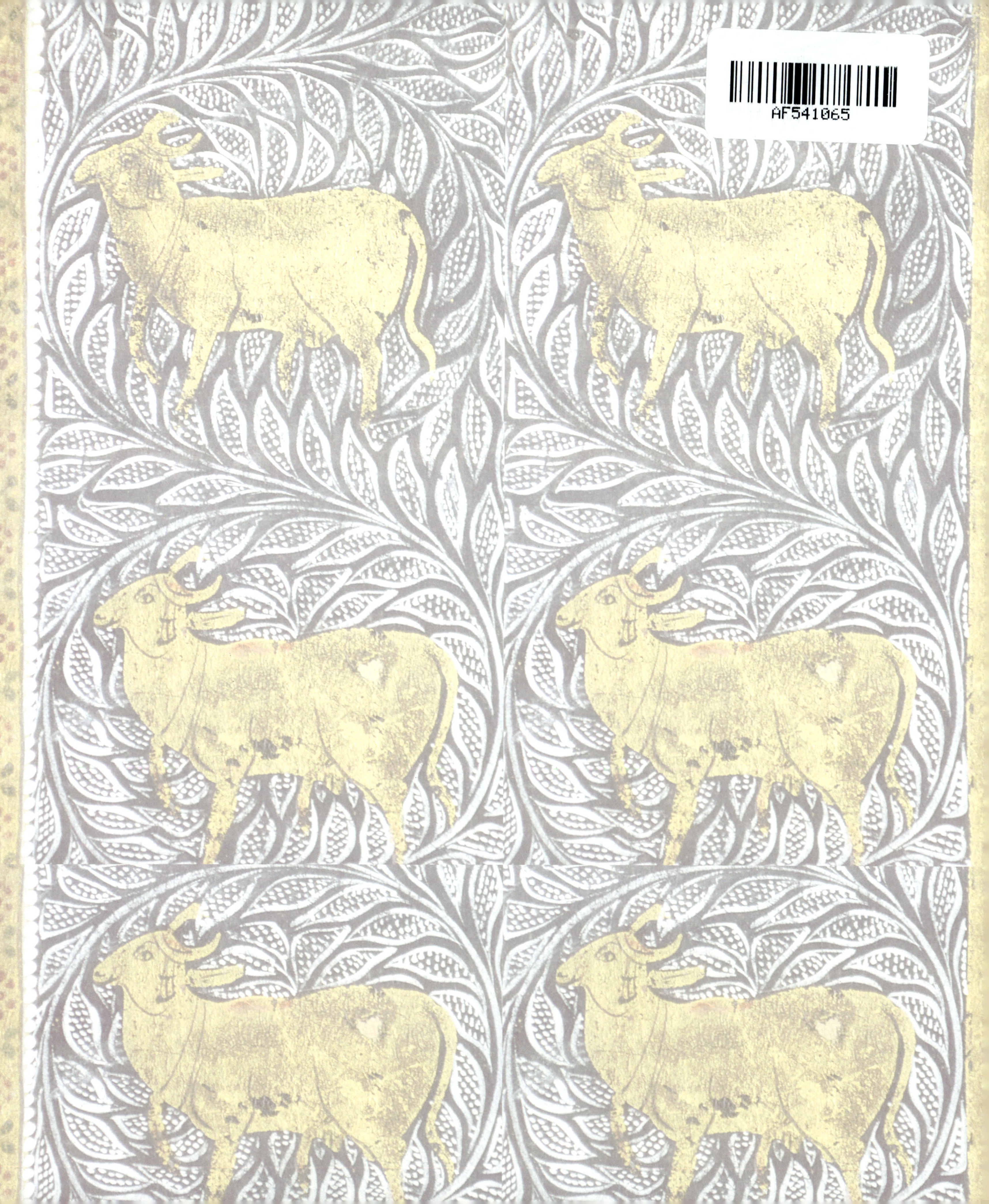

Portraits of Devotion

Popular *Manorath* Paintings from Nathdwara
in the Collection of Anil Relia

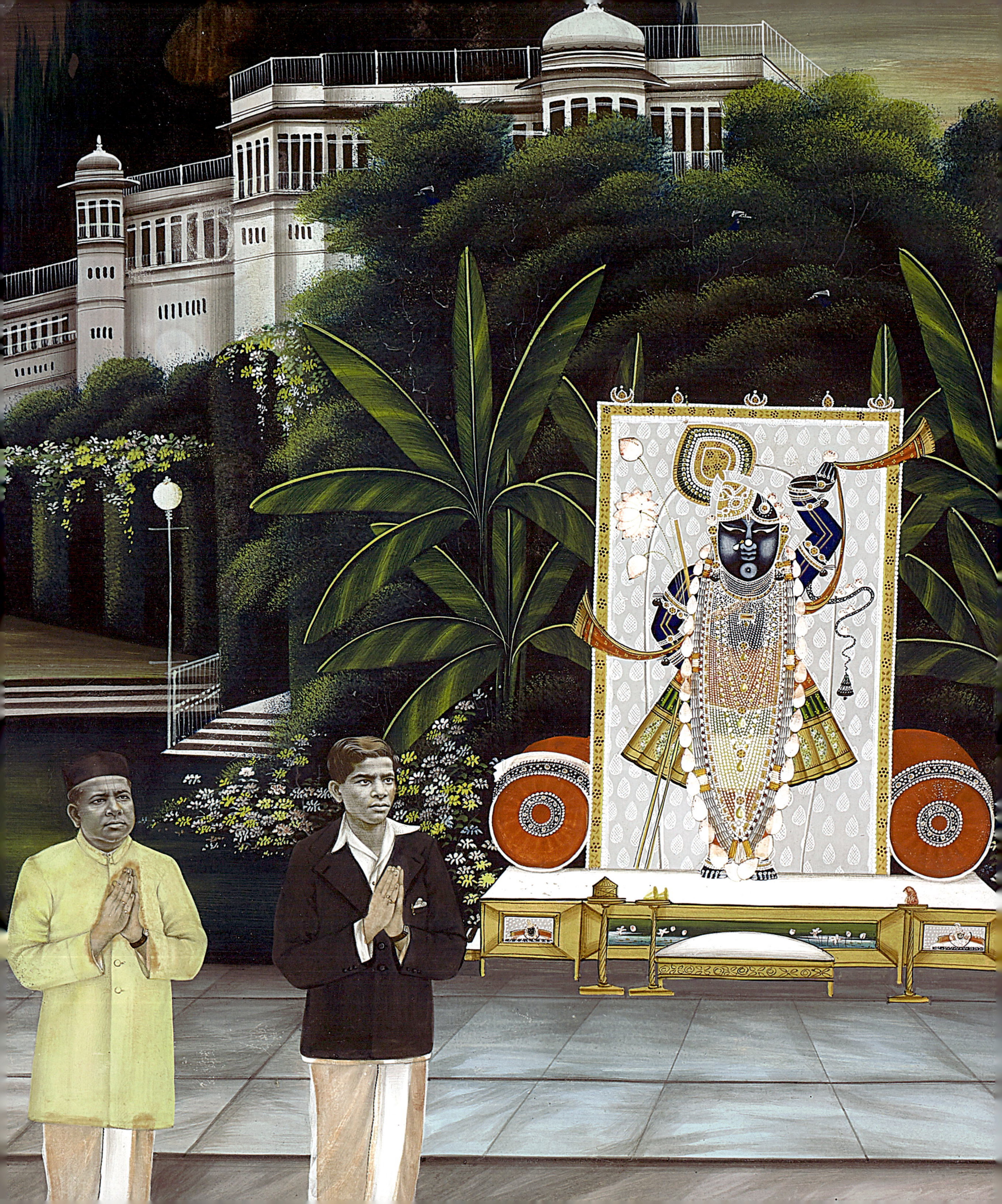

Portraits of Devotion

Popular *Manorath* Paintings from Nathdwara in the Collection of Anil Relia

Isabella Nardi

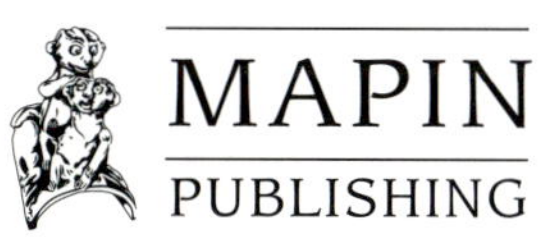

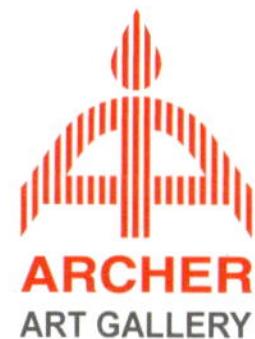

First published in India in 2019 by
Mapin Publishing Pvt. Ltd
706 Kaivanna, Panchvati, Ellisbridge
Ahmedabad 380006 INDIA
T: +91 79 40 228 228 • F: +91 79 40 228 201
E: mapin@mapinpub.com • www.mapinpub.com

in association with

Archer Art Gallery
2nd Floor, Phoenix
Near Vijay Cross Roads, Navrangpura
Ahmedabad 380009 INDIA
T: + 91 79 27413634 / 27413872
E: info@archerindia.com • www.archerindia.com

This catalogue has been published in conjunction with the exhibition 'Portraits of Devotion: Popular *Manorath* Paintings from Nathdwara in the Collection of Anil Relia' at Amdavad Ni Gufa, K. L. Campus, Navrangpura, Ahmedabad, March 2 to 10, 2019.

Text: Isabella Nardi
Photograph of the artworks: Cyrus Mobedji

ISBN: 978-93-85360-67-1 (Mapin)
ISBN: 978-81-931718-3-7 (Archer Art Gallery)

Copyediting and Proofreading: Mithila Rangarajan / Mapin Editorial
Design: Archer Graphic Studio
Design support: Gopal Limbad / Mapin Design Studio
Printed at Rajkalp Mudranalaya Private Limited, Lapkaman, Ahmedabad

CONTENTS

COLLECTOR'S NOTE

'Art' and 'Nathdwara' are two consistently recurring themes in my life. Somehow, both of them creep up in mysterious ways, leaving me in delight and curiosity. Together they generate a certain energy and response which make me want to know more or to experience something important in my life.

I have always liked collecting portraits and miniature paintings of the Nathdwara School. It was during one of my trips to acquire some portraits that I encountered *manorath* paintings. These works immediately attracted my attention due to their unusual visual elements, especially their photorealistic portraits. Most of these paintings were originally part of Pushti Marg popular culture and, therefore, they were not necessarily given much importance by scholars. Such paintings were commissioned by Pushti Marg devotees to keep an indelible record of a pilgrimage trip to Nathdwara. However, they were later disposed by their successive owners to find a new life with scrap dealers, antique sellers or at flea markets.

In 2002, after collecting a considerable number of works encompassing the wide variety of artistic genres produced at Nathdwara, I decided to exhibit them. I reached out to Amit Ambalal, who handpicked the paintings from my collection and identified the underlying theme for the exhibition. Together we curated a show titled 'Tasveer–How Camera Influenced Indian Portraiture', which included a couple of *manorath* paintings.

The process of collecting *manorath* paintings has led to a number of interesting anecdotes. A surprising incident happened in 2015, when I displayed a few *manorath*s from my collection in the 'Indian Portrait–VII' exhibition. During the show, a seventy-seven-year-old lady from Ahmedabad recognized her parents and herself in one of the *manorath* paintings on display (Cat. no. 28). She shared with me how they were frequent visitors to Nathdwara. During one of the trips, when she was eight years old, they went to an artist's studio to commission that particular work. The artist took a photograph of them which was used to produce the painting. The work was probably made to be donated to an institution to which her father was contributing as a wealthy philanthropist. In fact, she admitted, she never saw it in her house. Years later, I found that work through a scrap dealer and acquired it.

Through my experience, I have learnt that art can vivify our encounters in life, record them, examine them, reshape them, and finally, leave a trace that can be shared by others. Thus, I have always liked to reconstruct the history of Nathdwara painting through personal stories. I always get a thrill whenever I can identify the priests, nobles, or devotees portrayed in the paintings. One such incident occurred when I came across a *manorath* painting inscribed to the famous Nathdwara artist Champalal Hiralal (Cat. no. 5). I got immediately intrigued by it, not simply for its subject but because the devotee looked very familiar. It felt as if I knew that person and his face. Later on, going through my collection of sketches and drawings, I found a study of his portrait and immediately recognized the subject (Fig. 6). I was as elated as if I had met some acquaintance of mine after a long time.

In 2014, Isabella Nardi visited Ahmedabad while on her way to Jhalawar. At that time, she was researching the murals of the Garh-Mahal, many of which were executed by Nathdwara artists, including the famous Ghasiram. This is when I invited her to see my collection and I recounted to her my tryst with Nathdwara. After seeing my *manorath* paintings, she became instantly drawn to the subject and started exploring them more closely. A year later, she shared with me some of her findings which brought to the fore a story that needed to be told. In order to answer some of the new questions that emerged from her preliminary research, I decided to visit Nathdwara on numerous occasions to dialogue with some esteemed traditional artists and their families, including the relatives of Khubiram and Gopilal. This is how our vision on *manorath* painting expanded, leading to this catalogue which presents new discoveries on this intriguing devotional genre.

The collection in this catalogue is a way of seeing the world, a way of expression, and a way of bringing to the fore the latent. It is evident from these paintings that art equals life and life equals art.

Anil Relia

Ahmedabad, January 2019

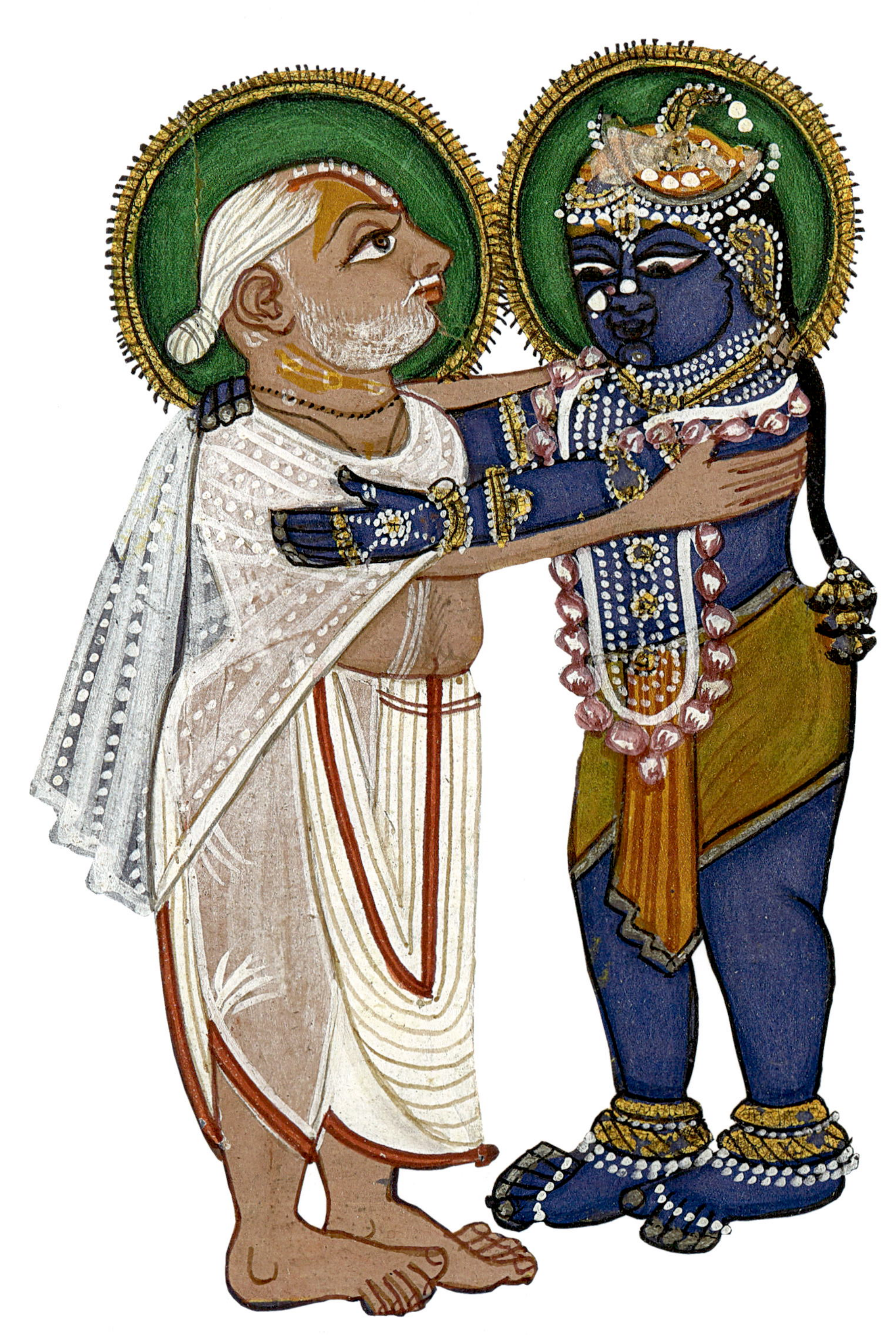

INTRODUCTION AND ACKNOWLEDGMENTS

The Krishnaite sect of Pushti Marg ("The Path of Grace"), also known by the name of Vallabha Sampradaya, originated at the end of the fifteenth century in the region of Braj, in modern-day Uttar Pradesh. In 1672, the sect moved to the town of Nathdwara, Rajasthan, which became its new headquarters. The town is celebrated not only for the so called *haveli* temple—a regal mansion that houses Pushti Marg's most revered icon, Shrinathji—but also for its distinctive school of painting. In Nathdwara, for about three centuries, traditional, hereditary lines of painters, residing in proximity to the temple, have created artefacts catering to the needs of Pushti Marg devotees and supporting the sect's rituals.

This monograph-cum-catalogue is an excursion into some of the devotional portraits that were commissioned in the twentieth century by Pushti Marg followers visiting their most important site of pilgrimage, Nathdwara. It concentrates on a particular genre that emerged in Nathdwara at the beginning of the twentieth century, which is commonly known as the *manorath*. Referred to in this catalogue by the more specific designation of "popular *manorath*s," works in this genre display distinct iconographic features: they portray Pushti Marg devotees next to Shrinathji, which is their most revered icon.[1]

Popular *manorath*s have occasionally appeared in catalogues of Nathdwara painting and books on Indian popular culture.[2] Most studies, however, have privileged more mainstream productions, such as the Nathdwara *pichhwai*s (temple hangings), for which this pilgrimage town is so famous. The present investigation is the first venture to place popular *manorath*s at the centre of an art historical enquiry and to consider them as a genre per se. This study makes no claims of exhausting the topic. Rather, it

1. For some more information on Pushti Marg and Shrinathji, see the Glossary.
2. For popular *manorath* images published in other sources, see Allana and Kumar 8; Ambalal, *Krishna as Shrinathji* 90; Dewan, *Embellished Reality*, cat. no. 24; Ghose, cat. no. 107; Krishna and Talwar 92, 212; Mitter, fig. 9; Pinney, "Stirred by Photography," fig. 3.13; Nanda 63; Robbins and Tokayer, fig. 14.13; and Ruia, figs. 1–13.

seeks to stimulate new debates and fresh research on marginalized art practices which have been overshadowed by mainstream narratives.

The catalogue is based on popular *manorath*s in the collection of Anil Relia, which is a distinguished and comprehensive archive of both traditional and contemporary South Asian art based in Ahmedabad.[3] The main thematic focus of the collection is portraiture, and, consistent with its geographic location, it holds a substantial concentration of works from Gujarat and Rajasthan, the lands where the cult of Shrinathji and its Pushti Marg network flourished. It is therefore not surprising to find among its holdings numerous artefacts from Nathdwara. The substantial number of popular *manorath*s held in the archive (currently thirty-five) makes for a concentration quite unique in any South Asian collection. These works provide significant information on the history of Nathdwara painting in the twentieth century—a time when transcultural agents, such as photography and academic realism, became integral parts of its organic development.

The present volume is divided into two parts: the first presents a contextual analysis of popular *manorath*s, and the second is a catalogue of thirty-five images. The analysis is subdivided into three chapters. The first presents a brief overview of the period in which popular *manorath*s flourished and emphasizes the importance of the Anil Relia collection in their study. It also highlights the lack of research on twentieth-century Nathdwara, the artistic production of which remains understudied. The second chapter provides a definition of the *manorath* genre and makes a subdivision between "traditional" and "popular" representations. In particular, this catalogue employs the word "traditional" to indicate those miniature paintings depicting intricate liturgical services officiated by a priest in front of a Pushti Marg icon, and the word "popular" to designate those images portraying Pushti Marg devotees attending a special ceremony of worship. While such images are similar in their iconography, they significantly differ in their meanings. The third chapter offers an analysis of popular *manorath* images illustrated in the catalogue, focusing on their techniques, styles, and iconographies. It also addresses some important elements that have emerged during our investigation, such as the ways of customizing the *manorath*s according to the commissioners' tastes, and the controversial practices of the Khubiram and Gopilal studio.

---

3. Many works in the collection of Anil Relia have been published in a series of catalogues. See, for example, Agarvwal; and Relia.

For the transcription of names—including those of historic figures, painters, and geographic locations—we have followed the anglicization common in other sources. The only exceptions are found in the catalogue's captions, where we have transliterated the Hindi and Gujarati inscriptions using diacritic marks. All illustrations in the catalogue are from the collection of Anil Relia. The text, however, refers to four images from other sources. I wish to thank Amit Ambalal for his permission to publish Fig. 4, Aditya Ruia for Fig. 11, and Vivek Nanda for Fig. 15. Fig. 2b is my own.

This publication would not have been possible without the contributions of many people. First and foremost, I wish to thank Anil Relia for opening the doors to his collection and providing access without encumbrance. I am also grateful for the generous hospitality I received from him and his entire family when I visited Ahmedabad in 2014 and 2017. I am indebted to Manan Relia for his constant assistance in answering my numerous questions, for providing precise information about the collection's holdings, and for supplying professional photographs. Many of these works are published here for the first time.

I would also like to thank Amit Ambalal for receiving me at his residence in Ahmedabad in 2017, for showing me parts of his collection, sharing his knowledge, and answering my numerous questions regarding Pushti Marg and *manorath* painting. I am grateful, as well, to Kay Talwar for helpful conversations and exchanges of information via email, and to the Udaipur-based artist Lalit Sharma for accompanying me to Nathdwara in 2014.

Part of this research was carried out while I was Visiting India Scholar at Cleveland State University in 2016. I wish to thank the Art Department there for hosting me and providing the resources needed for the project, and for sponsoring a fieldtrip to the Royal Ontario Museum (ROM) in Toronto. I am also grateful to the South Asian art curator at ROM, Deepali Dewan, for showing me the painted photographs in the collection and for discussing some of the crucial issues presented in this catalogue. Finally, parts of this research have been presented at international conferences and venues where I was fortunate to receive feedback that has undoubtedly improved my project and vision. Of course, all errors and shortcomings are my own.

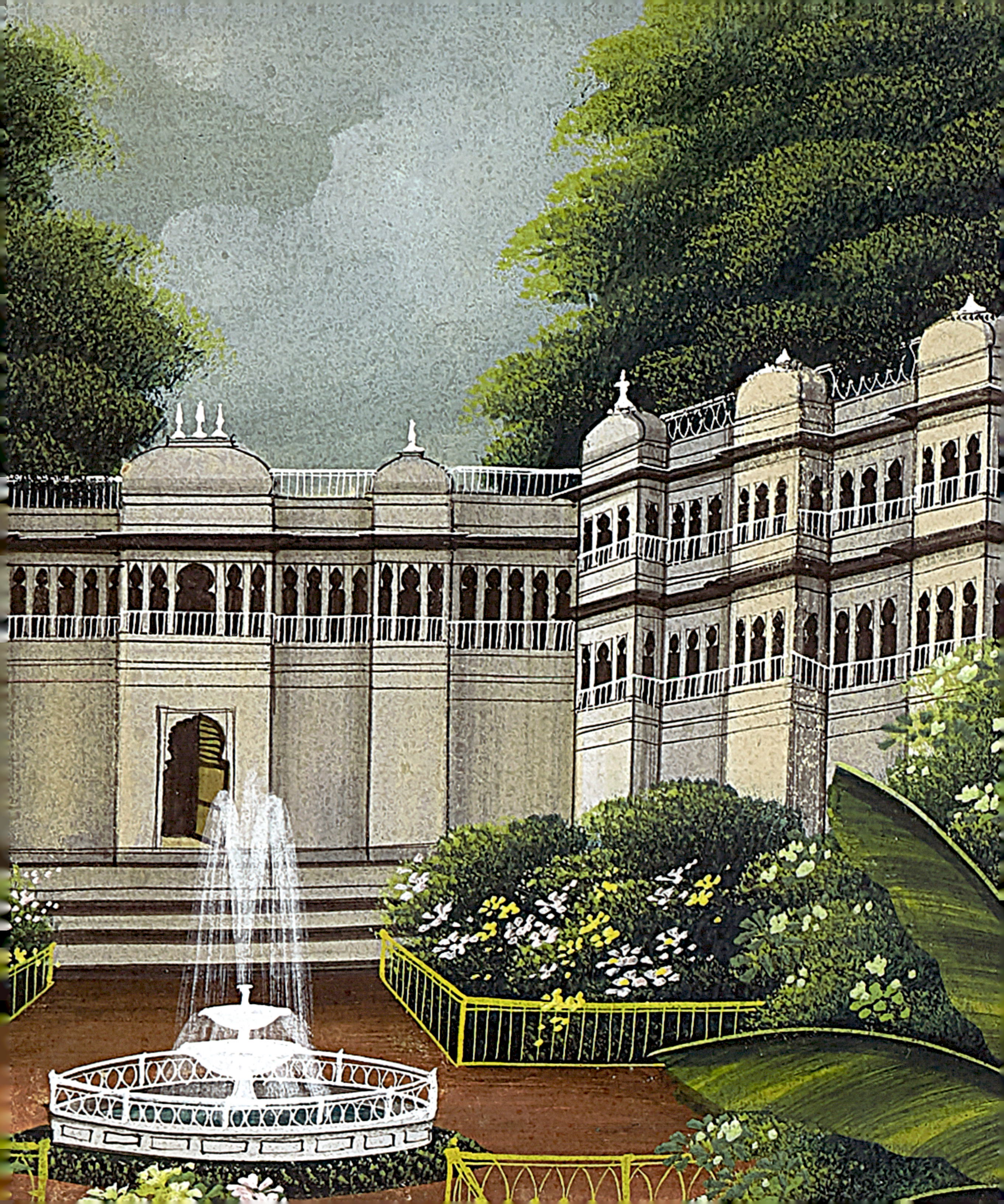

NATHDWARA PAINTING AND THE ANIL RELIA COLLECTION

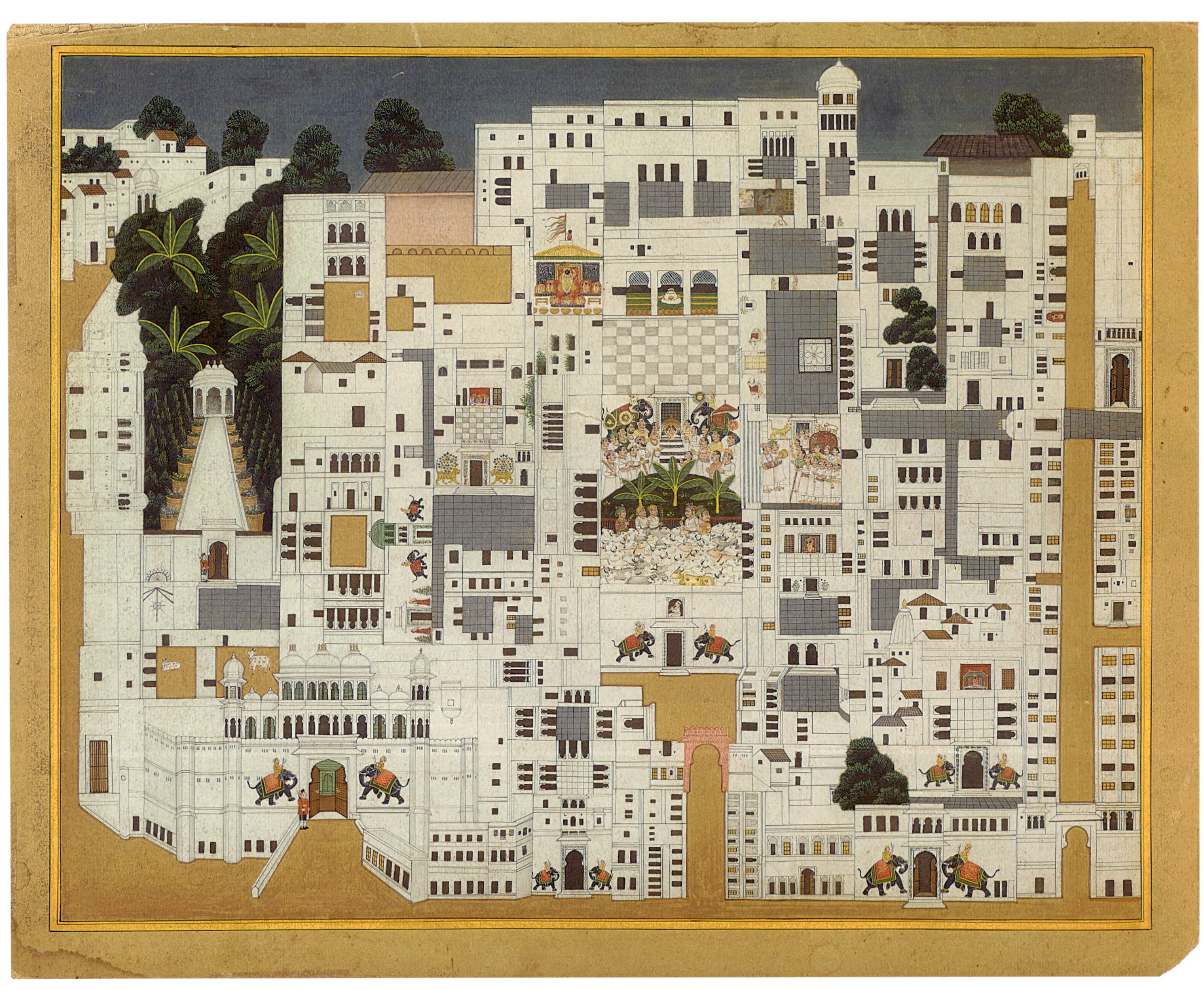

FIGURE 1A.

The *Haveli* Temple.
A traditional representation of the Nathdwara temple.

Opaque watercolour and gold on paper; c. 1900.
20.5 x 25.5 in (52.1 x 64.8 cm).

Nathdwara: an introduction

Shrinathji is the most important svarup, or self-manifested icon, of the Pushti Marg community.[4] This black marble statue, representing Krishna as a child, resides in the *haveli* temple of Nathdwara, a palatial mansion built in 1672. From the time of the temple's construction, the pilgrimage town of Nathdwara became the most important cultural centre of the Pushti Marg community (Fig. 1a).

Pushti Marg traces its origins to Mount Govardhan, in the region of Braj, where, in 1493, the icon of Shrinathji miraculously manifested itself to Vallabhacharya (1479–1531), the preceptor of the sect. Fig. 1b depicts the moment of the foundation of Pushti Marg—the first encounter and embrace between the philosopher Vallabhacharya and Shrinathji on Mount Govardhan. The black marble sculpture of Shrinathji is known to have resided in the region of Braj until 1669, when it was removed by its caretakers during a period of political instability in the region. After two years of peregrinations in Rajasthan, the icon found its new abode in the town of Nathdwara.[5]

FIGURE 1B.

Pratham Milan.
The first encounter of Vallabhacharya with Shrinathji at Mount Govardhan.
Opaque watercolour and gold on paper; c. 1840.
7.1 x 10 in. (18 x 25.4 cm).

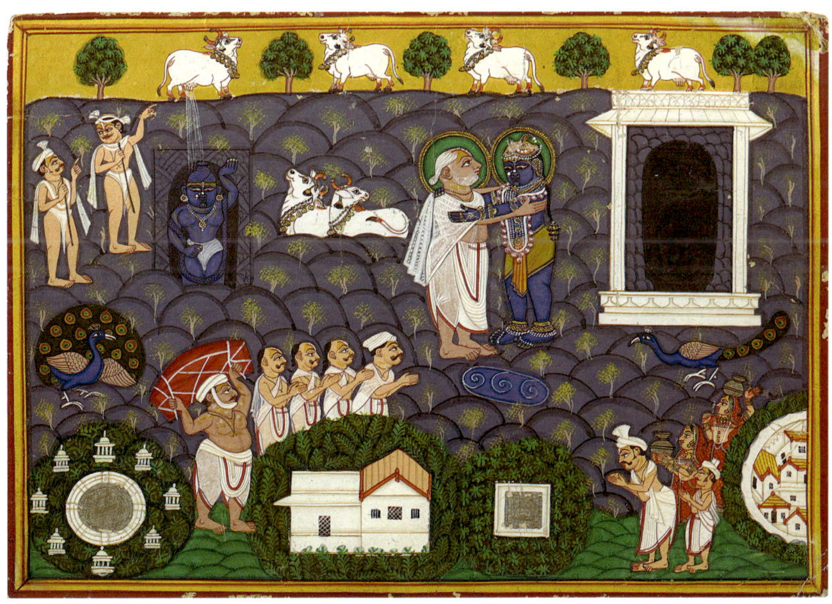

The foundation of the *haveli* temple in 1672 became the catalyst shaping the future of Nathdwara and of the Pushti Marg community in the region. Devotional activities in the town were not limited to complex liturgical celebrations; they also included the production and patronage of music,

4. For a definition of *svarup*, see the Glossary.

5. For more information on the sect of Pushti Marg, see Barz. For the manifestation of the Shrinathji icon on Mount Govardhan, see Vaudeville. For the reasons for Shrinathji's exile from Braj, see Pauwels and Bachrach.

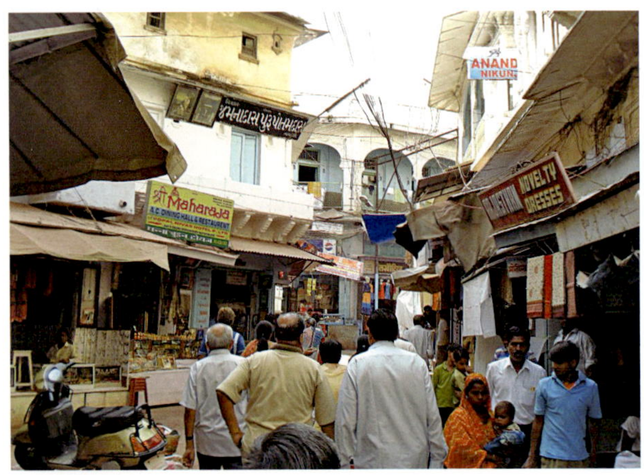

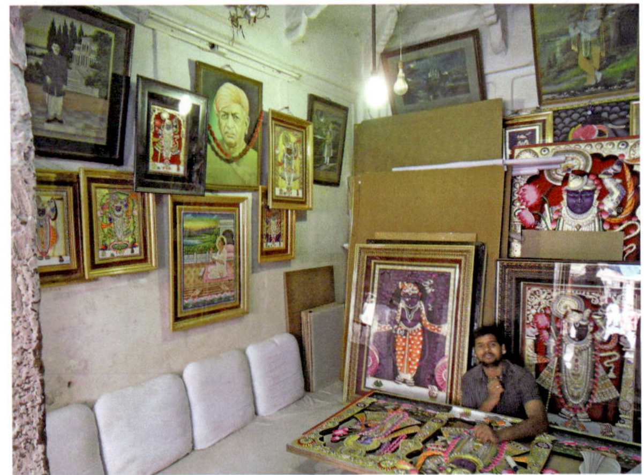

FIGURE 2A.

A Street in the Bazar of Nathdwara.
On the left is the Jamnadas Purusottamdas studio; next to its board on the wall there is a *manorath* painting and another devotional image.

Photograph by Anil Relia, 2005.

FIGURE 2B.

The Workshop of Artist Khubiram and Sons.
Displayed on the walls are old memorial portraits and modern representations of Shrinathji.

Photograph by Isabella Nardi, 2014.

literature, and the visual arts.[6] These arts were traditionally promoted by the *tilkayat*s, or head priests, of the Shrinathji temple.[7] This patronage was considered a way of performing *seva*, or devotional service, to the icon. Among the traditional arts, painting became particularly popular. The origins of this distinctive school have been traced back to the very foundation of the temple, and it has been carried out by a network of traditional painters from that time up to the present day (Figs. 2a, 2b).[8]

One of the most popular artefacts produced at Nathdwara is the temple hanging commonly called the *pichhwai*: a painting on cloth designed to be hung behind a sacred icon during a temple ritual. Its liturgical function is suggested by its name, which derives from the Hindi word *pichhe* ("behind" or "at the rear") and which can be translated loosely as "backdrop." Traditionally, temple hangings were commissioned by the *haveli* temple to be placed behind the icon of Shrinathji during the celebration of special festivals. They were used to produce a particular atmosphere within the *nij mandir*, or sanctum. The decorative motifs on the *pichhwai*s were conceived to stimulate a particular set of emotions and evoke specific memories in the worshippers. For example, a Gopashtami *pichhwai*, which is adorned with a herd of cows arranged geometrically on the surface of the painting, would have been used for the commemoration of the first time Krishna went grazing the cows—that is, for the Gopashtami Festival.[9]

Nathdwara is also famous for traditional miniature painting on paper. Popular themes include Krishna's *lila*s (or Krishna's adventures as a child), portraits, and representations of the icon of Shrinathji adorned for temple celebrations. In these illustrations, Shrinathji is often depicted in the company of the head priest and

6. For a study of the musical tradition at the Shrinathji temple, see Gaston. For studies of Nathdwara visual arts see, for example, Skelton; Lyons; Krishna and Talwar; Ghose; Ambalal, *Krishna as Shrinathji*; and Pinney, *Photos of the Gods* 80–104.
7. *Tilkayat* is the title of the head priest of the Nathdwara temple. Other priests of the Pushti Marg community are usually known by the name of *goswami* or *maharaj*.
8. For the origins of Nathdwara painting and some of its earliest examples, see Ambalal, "The *Tilkayats* as Patrons." For the network of Nathdwara painters and their genealogies, see Lyons.
9. For more information on *pichhwai* painting, see Skelton; Ambalal, *Krishna as Shrinathji* 76–79; Krishna and Talwar; and Ghose. For a list of festivals in which *pichhwai*s are used, see Ambalal, *Krishna as Shrinathji* 163–164. For more information on the term *pichhwai* and its uses, see Goswamy and Goswamy 41–42.

other religious or royal figures. Fig. 3, for example, illustrates a special event ceremoniously officiated in 1908 by Tilkayat Govardhanlal (1862–1934), the head priest of the *haveli* temple. A detailed analysis of this painting and its ritual intricacies will be presented later.

The collection of Anil Relia: focus and significance

Our knowledge of the arts of Nathdwara has been shaped by the study of prestigious collections. These include the Collection of Karl Mann, now at the Freer and Sackler galleries in Washington, D.C., the Tapi Collection in Surat, and the collections of the Calico Museum, the Sarabhai Foundation, and Amit Ambalal, all of which are located in Ahmedabad.[10] These archives mostly concentrate on miniature paintings and *pichhwai*s depicting devotional themes produced in the period that stretches from the eighteenth to the early twentieth century. This selection of media and genres, shaped by particular collectors' interests, provides a partial knowledge of the visual arts scenario in Nathdwara. A more comprehensive overview is offered by Tryna Lyons's study. Her book concentrates on the personal collections of living traditional artists in the region and on the special commissions executed by their descendants for both royal and religious patrons. Her study includes a variety of works, such as *pichhwai*s, paintings, sketchbooks, and murals, up to the mid-twentieth century.

In this context, the collection of Anil Relia offers to play an important role in integrating our knowledge. Its complementary narrative of the artistic scenario in Nathdwara not only covers a longer historical span, from the eighteenth up to the late twentieth century; it also presents a much wider array of media and genres. Moreover, an inspection of the collection immediately reveals a subsidiary narrative to the mainstream discourse delineated above. Its holdings suggest that Nathdwara experienced a remarkable flourishing of the arts in the period that stretches from the late nineteenth to the mid-twentieth century. The plethora of works from this period is not limited to the classic production of *pichhwai*s and miniature paintings; it also includes mixed-media paintings, prints, collages, and black-and-white and painted photographs. The crucial artistic period that the collection of Anil Relia highlights

10. For the Collection of Karl Mann, see Skelton. For the Tapi Collection, see Krishna and Talwar. For the collection of the Calico Museum and the Sarabhai Foundation, see Goswamy and Goswamy. For the Collection of Amit Ambalal, see Ambalal, *Krishna as Shrinathji*.

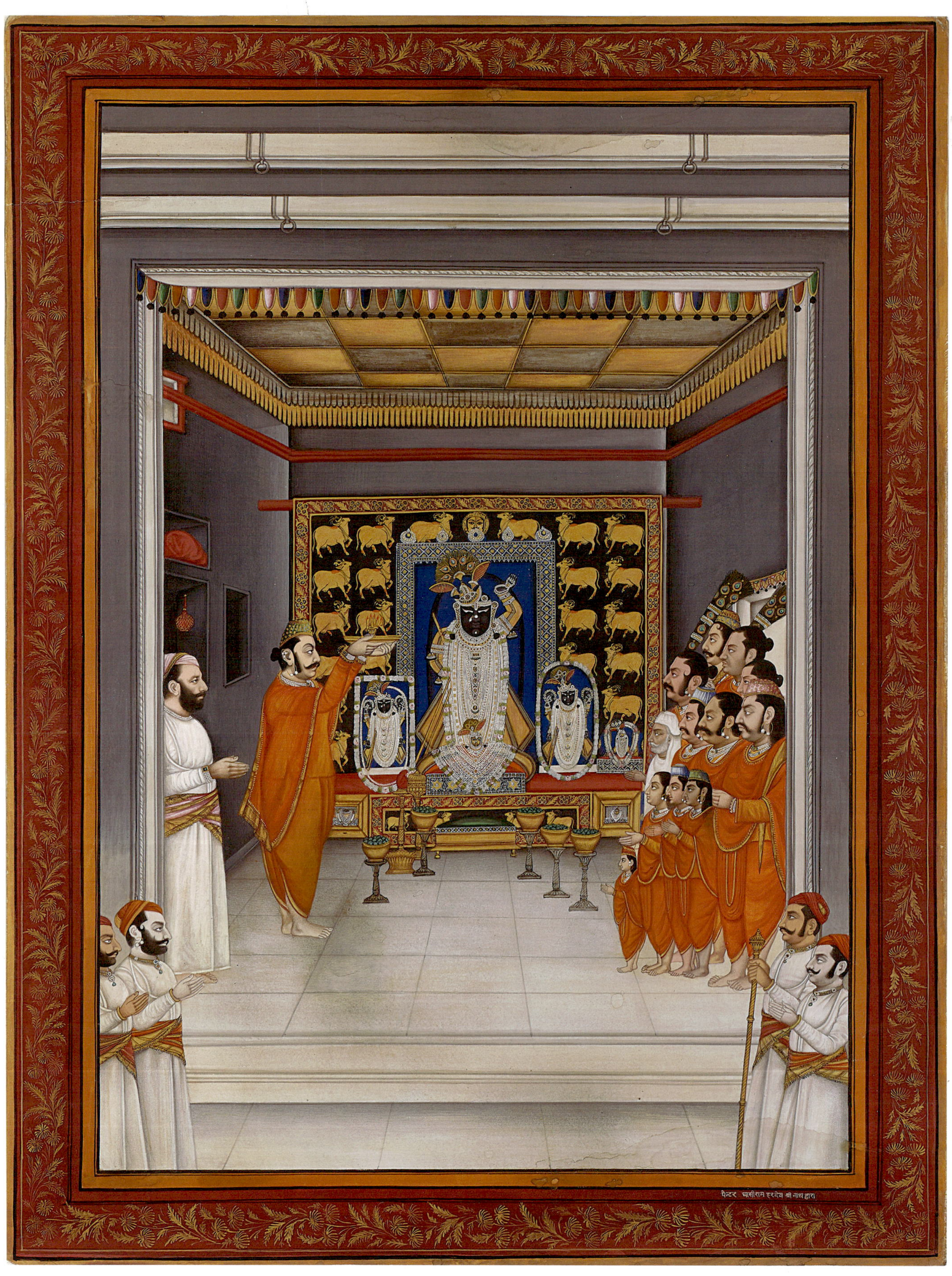
पेन्टर घासीराम हरदेव श्री नाथ द्वारा

Figure 3.
Festival of the Five *Svarups*.
By Ghasiram Hardev Sharma;
opaque watercolour and gold on paper;
c. 1908.
21.1 x 15.9 in. (53.6 x 40.5 cm).

corresponds to a reinvigoration of the arts at the hands of an influential priest, Tilkayat Govardhanlal, who was the head of the Shrinathji temple from 1876 until his death in 1934. This local revitalization corresponds, in turn, to other movements of cultural and artistic revival across the subcontinent in the late colonial period.

Nathdwara painting at the time of Govardhanlal

The flourishing of the arts at the time of Govardhanlal (1862–1934) came on the heels of an unfortunate period in the history of Pushti Marg, in which the sect suffered a substantial loss of credibility. This decline began with the notorious Libel Case of 1862, in which the head priest of the Shri Balkrishnaji Temple of Surat, a temple in the network of Pushti Marg, was convicted of sexual misconduct.[11] This disturbing event was followed, in 1876, by the exile from Nathdwara for insubordination of the *tilkayat* of the Shrinathji temple, Girdharji (also spelled Giridhar, 1843–1903), who was accused of extorting money from pilgrims to support his luxurious lifestyle. His conduct violated the sect's precepts, which oblige Pushti Marg priests to dedicate themselves fully to devotional service, or *seva*. For his improper behavior, Girdharji was exiled in the region of Braj on May 21, 1876. Despite his numerous petitions to the Mewar Government, he never succeeded in attaining reinstatement. Instead, his son Govardhanlal, then a minor, was appointed *tilkayat* of the *haveli* temple.[12]

The appointment of Govardhanlal in 1876 coincided with the revocation of the 1809 edict in which the State of Mewar had accorded the *tilkayat*s of Nathdwara full control over their judicial, administrative, and economic affairs. From 1876 on, these matters fell under the control of the State of Mewar, leaving Govardhanlal full authority over the religious functions of the temple. This important change in administration allowed the priest a considerable amount of time to look after the well-being of the community. This new emphasis was obviously accompanied by a significant amount of pressure to restore the credibility lost by Pushti Marg in the wake of the exile of his father.

Govardhanlal promoted new projects to relaunch Nathdwara as a devotional centre. He built a Sanskrit school, a public library, and hospitals, and he put a great deal

11. For the Libel Case of 1862, see Mulji 170–182, Appendix.
12. For the misbehavior of Girdharji, see Jindel 23–24, 197–199; and Saha.

of effort into boosting the arts, especially literature, music, and painting. He also focused on the organization of important religious celebrations, such as the Festival of the Five *Svarups* of 1908 (Fig. 3), a reunion of five major icons of Pushti Marg in the *haveli* temple, intended as a way of reinforcing the network of the sect in the region and increasing its power. On a transregional level, this renewed interest in religious celebrations also corresponded to a wider revival of such activities in the colonial period across the entire subcontinent.[13]

The Festival of the Five *Svarups* was meant to invoke a lost age of prosperity and splendour under Tilkayat Damodarji II (1797–1826), one of the most prominent priests in the history of Nathdwara, known for the organization of one of the most legendary events of the sect, the Festival of the Seven *Svarups*, in 1822.[14] On that occasion, Damodarji II managed to reunite seven Pushti Marg icons in the *haveli* temple. Govardhanlal's 1908 festival (Fig. 3), which emulated the grandeur of the 1822 celebrations, was organized to re-establish the popularity and integrity of the sect. He largely succeeded in his task, becoming for his efforts a prominent and esteemed figure. The significant number of portraits of Govardhanlal sold to the pilgrims at Nathdwara are an indication of the reputation he built during his lifetime.[15]

The catalogue

Out of the vast number of Nathdwara artefacts in the collection of Anil Relia, this study will concentrate on a smaller selection of works called popular *manoraths*. Early examples of popular *manoraths* date to the beginning of the twentieth century, the period of Govardhanlal's efforts to revive devotional activities, and they have remained a favorite genre even until recently.[16] The narrow focus of this catalogue has been chosen because popular *manorath* images, which are generously enough represented in Anil Relia's collection to allow an in-depth examination, represent such a distinctive feature of the artistic production of Nathdwara. This is not to say

13. For the revival of community festivals and processions in the late colonial period, see K. Jain 111–112.
14. For an analysis of the Festival of the Seven *Svarups*, see Nardi, "La Miniatura come Documento Storico."
15. The collection of Anil Relia holds a significant number of portraits of Govardhanlal. For a catalogue entirely dedicated to this subject, see Relia.
16. For a studio photograph, dated c. 1994, which replicates popular *manorath* conventions, see Pinney, *Photos of the Gods*, fig. 72.

that images of devotees with their personal deities were not common elsewhere in India; however, the development of a fully-fledged genre of pilgrimage images, with its own specific iconography, which was practiced for almost a century, is unique to this context.[17] Thus far, only one essay has focused on this subject; in it, the renowned artist, collector, and scholar Amit Ambalal introduces a set of notions that this catalogue seeks to elaborate more fully.[18] While Ambalal's study serves as a foundation, the present investigation considerably expands upon his treatment of the *manorath* genre, defining its origins, significance, techniques, and iconographies. It is hoped that our attention to this little-known subject will spark new interest in Nathdwara and its historical connections with the wider context of South Asian arts.

17. Paintings of devotees next to a divine figure are also common in other traditions. For some examples from South India, see Dallapiccola et al., figs. 2.7, 9.3–9.5. In a totally different context, for a remarkable parallel of pilgrimage photographs, which developed in the holy city of Mashhad in Iran, see Eshaghi. I wish to thank Christiane Gruber for pointing this study out to me (personal communication, June 2018).

18. See Ambalal, "*Manoratha* Paintings."

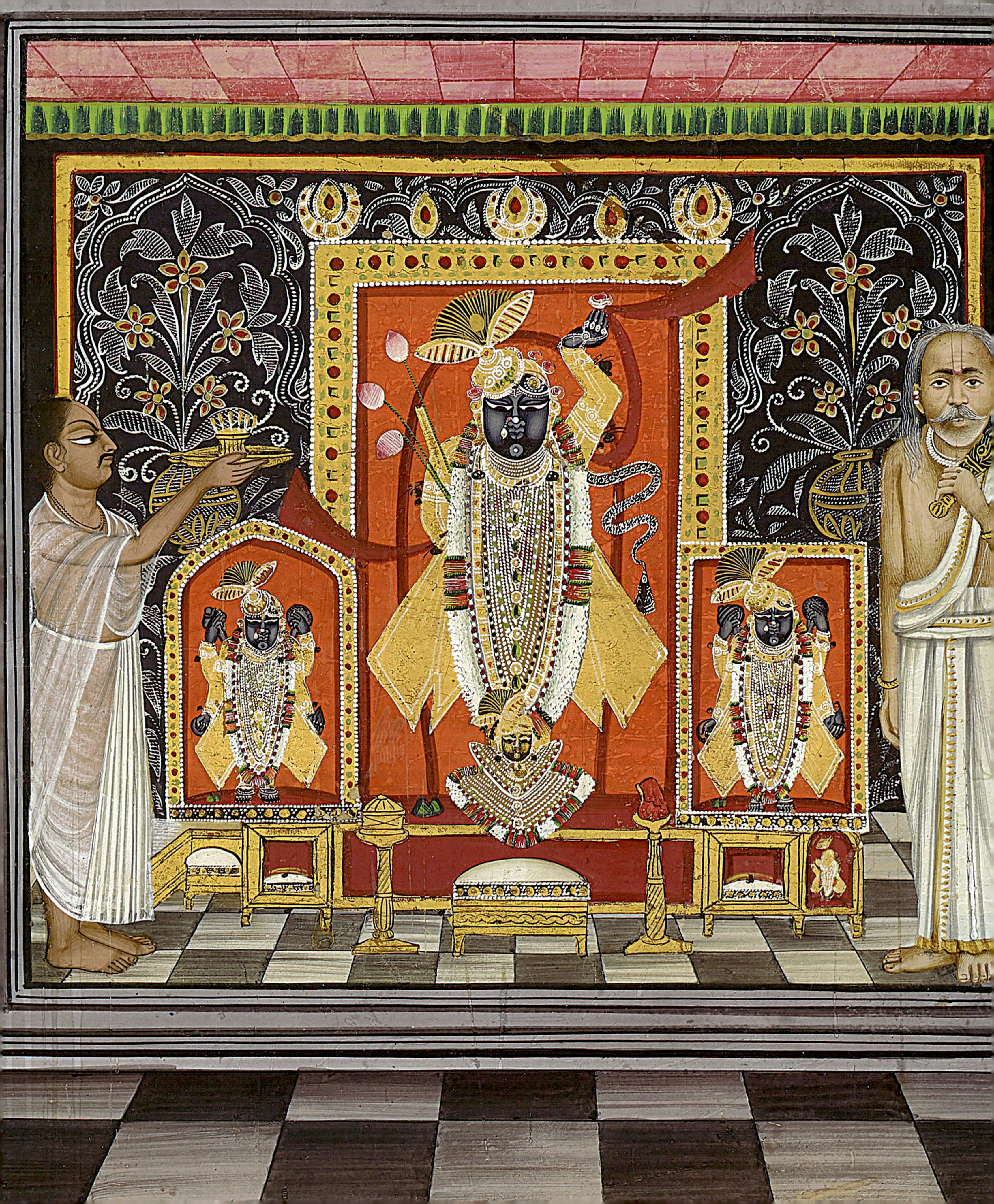

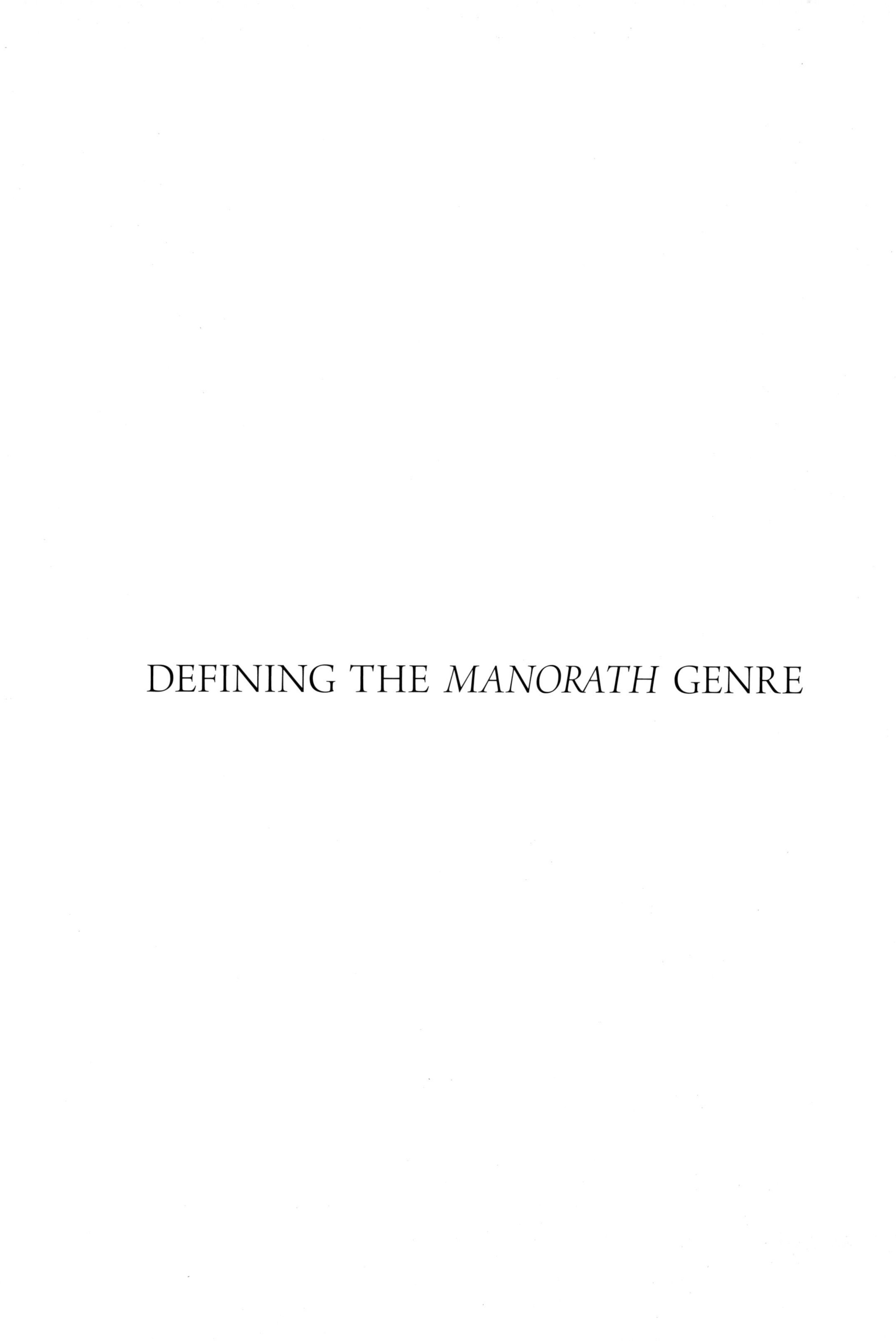

DEFINING THE *MANORATH* GENRE

Definitions of *manorath*

The term *manorath* derives from the Sanskrit word *manoratha,* which literally means "mind's vehicle." The term has been loosely translated as "heart's joy," "desire," "heart-felt wish," and "cherished purpose or aim."[19] In Pushti Marg devotional practices, this "desire" is associated with the aspiration of giving and receiving from God during *darshan, darshan* being that occasion when a worshipper has the opportunity of seeing and being seen by the divinity while visiting a temple. At that time, the devotee will beseech something from the deity.

Accordingly, in visual art from Nathdwara, a *manorath* image is a representation of this aspiration of entering into mutual communication with a Pushti Marg icon, such as Shrinathji. In the context of art history, the term *manorath* has usually been employed to designate images depicting a ceremony in front of Shrinathji. The present study, however, suggests that such loose terminology is in need of further clarification. An iconographic analysis reveals that there are in fact two different types of *manorath*s: there are "traditional" *manorath*s, which are miniature paintings with a liturgical focus (Fig. 3), and "popular" *manorath*s, which concentrate on the corporeal experience of the pilgrim in the presence of Shrinathji or any other Pushti Marg icon. The images in this catalogue belong to the category of the popular *manorath,* which developed in the early twentieth century as an evolution of its traditional counterpart. At this point, a more detailed explication of the two different types becomes necessary, since, although they are visually similar, they diverge significantly in their meanings.

19. See Monier-Williams 785; and McGregor 791.

Traditional *manoraths*

A traditional *manorath* represents a ceremony officiated by a priest in front of a Pushti Marg icon, typically Shrinathji. Paintings representing this theme had a long history in the Nathdwara visual repertoire, which is why the word "traditional" is apt to describe them.[20] These were commissioned and collected by a variety of Pushti Marg audiences, including such elites as priests and royals as well as followers of the sect.

Traditional *manorath*s centre on scenes of particular priests officiating in special worship services before Pushti Marg icons, following a combination of liturgical prescriptions and personal inclinations. Such opportunities are only accorded to a small number of privileged religious figures. As Amit Ambalal explains, it is the aspiration of every Pushti Marg priest to perform a ritual to Shrinathji, which is the most important icon of the sect. Ambalal also explains that to perform a *manorath* means "to fulfil a long cherished desire, a dream, and the innermost yearning to perform *seva* to the deity in one's own way."[21] Such a ceremony would consist in decorating the icon, hanging a *pichhwai* behind it, arranging flowers, having special foods prepared for the occasion, singing poetry, and performing other practices common to the *seva* tradition of the sect.

One example of a traditional *manorath* is the painting depicting the Festival of the Five *Svarup*s (Fig. 3). This painting portrays in great detail a special event which was officiated by Tilkayat Govardhanlal in 1908.[22] The painting indicates that this was not an ordinary observance at the Nathdwara temple: the commemoration was graced by the presence of four exceptional visitors, which made the event memorable. These special guests are four Pushti Marg icons, or *svarup*s, which were gathered next to Shrinathji in the sanctum of the *haveli* temple.[23] It is useful to remember that *svarup*s are considered and treated as living beings and that we must, therefore, view them as active participants in the festival. This function was also attended by the ruler of Mewar, Maharana Fateh Singh (r. 1884–1930), and by other Pushti Marg priests.

---

20. For an early composition, dated to c. 1772, see Ghose, cat. no. 31.
21. See Ambalal, "*Manoratha* Paintings" 214–215.
22. Two paintings representing the same subject are found in the collection of Amit Ambalal and published in Ambalal, "*Manoratha* Paintings," figs. 18.3–18.4.
23. The total number of *svarup*s, or self-manifested icons of Pushti Marg, is nine. For their names and present locations, see the term *svarup* in the Glossary.

The *svarups* are identifiable by their iconographic features. In the centre top is Shrinathji, which dominates the group in size and position. This black marble sculpture is recognizable by its left arm raised in the act of lifting Mount Govardhan. At its feet is the small metal icon of Navnitpriyaji, a form representing Krishna as a child with a ball of butter in one hand. On the left of Shrinathji is the black marble icon of Dwarkadishji of Kankroli, identifiable by its four arms and by the square top of its stele. On the right is Mathureshji of Kota with four arms and round-topped stele. On the far right of the group is the metal statue of Vitthalnathji, a Pushti Marg icon also residing at Nathdwara, but in a separate temple.

Fig. 3 indicates the "desire" and the capabilities expressed by Govardhanlal in organizing this festival with all its grand pomp and ceremony. A liturgical celebration of this caliber would have required great diplomatic and organizational skills: inviting other Pushti Marg icons to travel to the *haveli* temple of Nathdwara would have entailed intricate negotiations and agreements with their caretakers. This is one of the reasons why such special visits were rare. A precursor of this occasion was the famed Festival of the Seven *Svarups* of 1822, which has already been mentioned. Priests acquired *karmic* merit and personal prestige from coordinating such exceptional events.

Popular *manoraths*

The expression "popular" adopted in this catalogue refers to the network of Pushti Marg devotees.[24] Their milieu and arena of action were notably different from those of the elites (priests and royals) of Rajasthan. A popular *manorath* is an image commissioned by a devotee, which narrates his own personal experience of participating in a ritual performance. These images, illustrating worshippers in the presence of Shrinathji, had a deep emotional significance for them because they embodied both the corporeal pilgrimage to Nathdwara and the inner devotional experience.

An important example of a popular *manorath* is Fig. 4.[25] Entitled *Mantubai's Manorath of Sanjhi*, this intricate work was executed by Champalal Hiralal Gaur (c. 1875–1930)

24. For a discussion on the different variations in which the term "popular" has been used in the context of Indian popular culture, see K. Jain 118.

25. This is also published in Ambalal, "*Manoratha* Paintings," fig. 18.6; Lyons, figs. 109–110; and Ghose, cat. no. 106. For a detailed description of the painting, see Lyons 117–119.

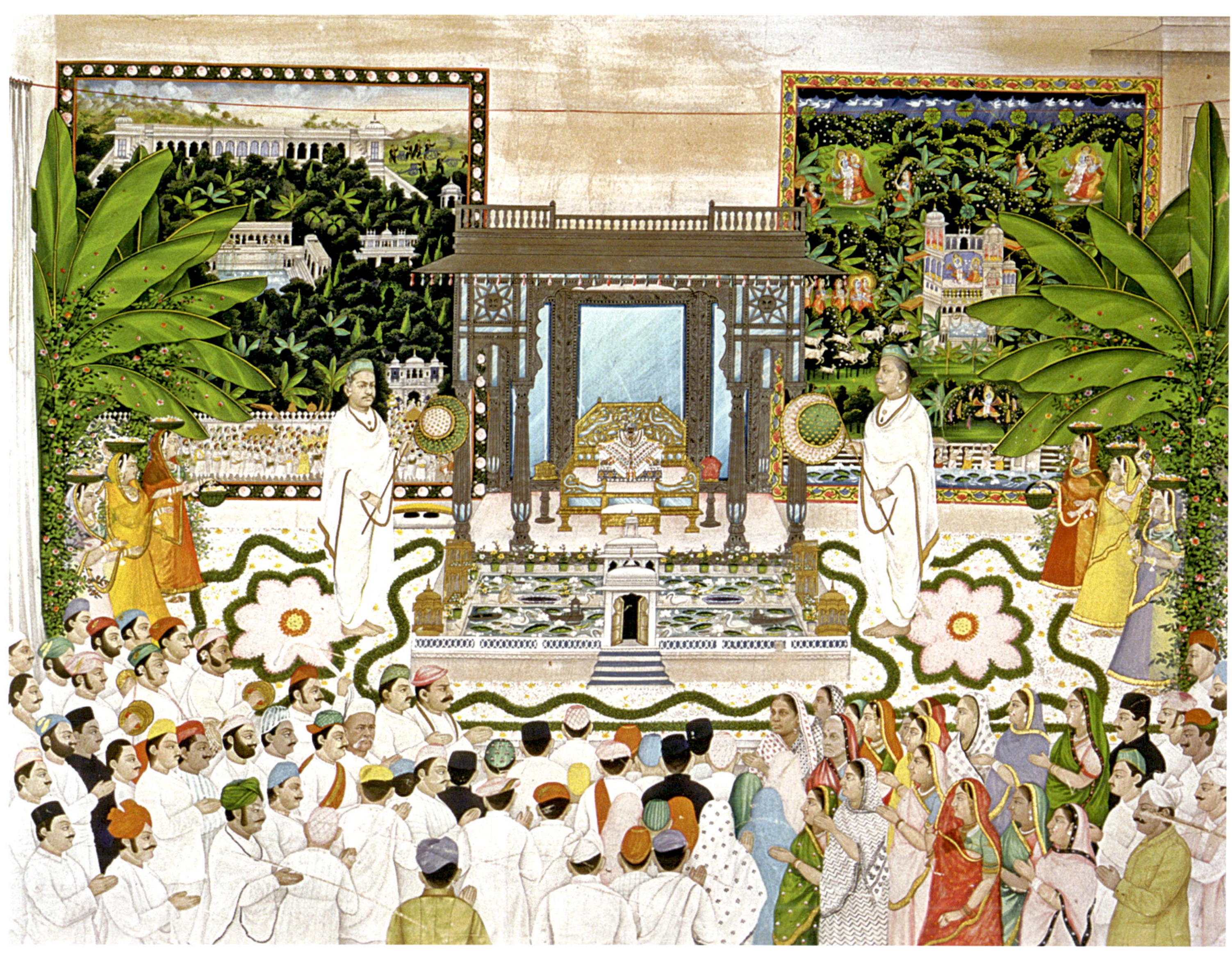

FIGURE 4.
Mantubai's Manorath of Sanjhi.
By Champalal Hiralal Gaur;
opaque watercolour, gold and silver on paper; dated 1915.
16.15 x 21 in. (41 x 53.5 cm).
Courtesy of Amit Ambalal.

in 1915, having been commissioned by a wealthy woman named Mantubai. Her name appears in a long inscription at the bottom of the painting, which identifies her as the patron of this opulent celebration. Her photo-realistic likeness appears in the lower centre of the composition.

The sumptuous celebrations are illustrated in great detail. They were performed in front of the icon of Navnitpriyaji in a courtyard of the *haveli* temple. The small metal icon of Navnitpriyaji has been placed on a golden throne under a silver canopy. The ceremony is officiated by Govardhanlal, standing on the right, and by his son, Damodarlal (1897–1936), on the left. The commemoration is taking place on a platform decorated by an intricate *sanjhi*, which is a design made of flowers, petals and leaves. Its meandering arrangement on the white marble floor suggests the flowing of the Yamuna river in the region of Braj, the land where Krishna spent his childhood. To evoke this locale there are also wooden mannequins representing the *gopi*s, or cowherd girls, carrying flowers in baskets on their heads, a lotus pond placed in front of the golden throne, and, hanging on the rear wall, two *pichhwai*s depicting gardens with lush vegetation.

While Fig. 4 depicts a splendid liturgical celebration officiated by Govardhanlal, the image closely relates to the personal experience of Mantubai and to her "desire" of sponsoring such a ritual. Making a donation to the *haveli* of Shrinathji was a common way to commemorate important family events, such as births, weddings, and deaths.[26] Mantubai, who was the widow of a rich merchant from Mumbai, was paying homage to her deceased husband by sponsoring this sumptuous ritual. Such an important event was worth immortalizing in a painting to make it even more memorable.

In Pushti Marg, the offering of gifts to temples and their icons was also a way to flaunt one's own prosperity.[27] The opulent display of riches was performed with the objective of pleasing Shrinathji, an intention which was also met by considering and treating the icon as a living child.[28] In return, the devotee would receive *pushti*, or grace. This aspect of reciprocity is fundamental to Pushti Marg ritual practices. In time, this interdependence affirmed the potency of icons, which were believed to be capable of fulfilling the devotees' wishes. As Peabody further explains, one of the canonical texts of the sect, the *Shrinathji ki Prakatya Varta*, "recounts how the statue of Shrinathji satisfied numerous entreaties of devotees, such as curing infertility, finding brides for sons, returning lost cattle, and restoring good health" (58). For this reason, pilgrims traveled long distances to communicate their wishes directly to Shrinathji and to give donations.

The popular *manorath* image is not, therefore, merely a souvenir of a pilgrimage trip; it represents a transaction with the deity. It is a visual depiction of a pilgrim's experience in taking *darshan* of Shrinathji and in attending a special ceremony in which he will make his wishes known to the deity. In popular *manorath*s, the devotees

26. See Shah 47.

27. See Peabody 106.

27. See Toomey 168.

are represented as patrons, not as mere observers of a function, and their likenesses become essential features of the composition. Not all pilgrims, however, had the economic means to sponsor such lavish ceremonies as Mantubai did. Indeed, most of them would have donated relatively small sums of money, and the images they commissioned were generally not as intricate as the one shown in Fig. 4, which is indeed an outstanding and costly work. Many of the popular *manorath*s in the present catalogue do not display the artistic intricacies of Fig. 4, but rather they are characterized by some compositional homogeneity. This uniformity was the result of a semi-mechanized process of execution which was developed in response to the increasing demand for *manorath* images, especially from the 1930s onward.

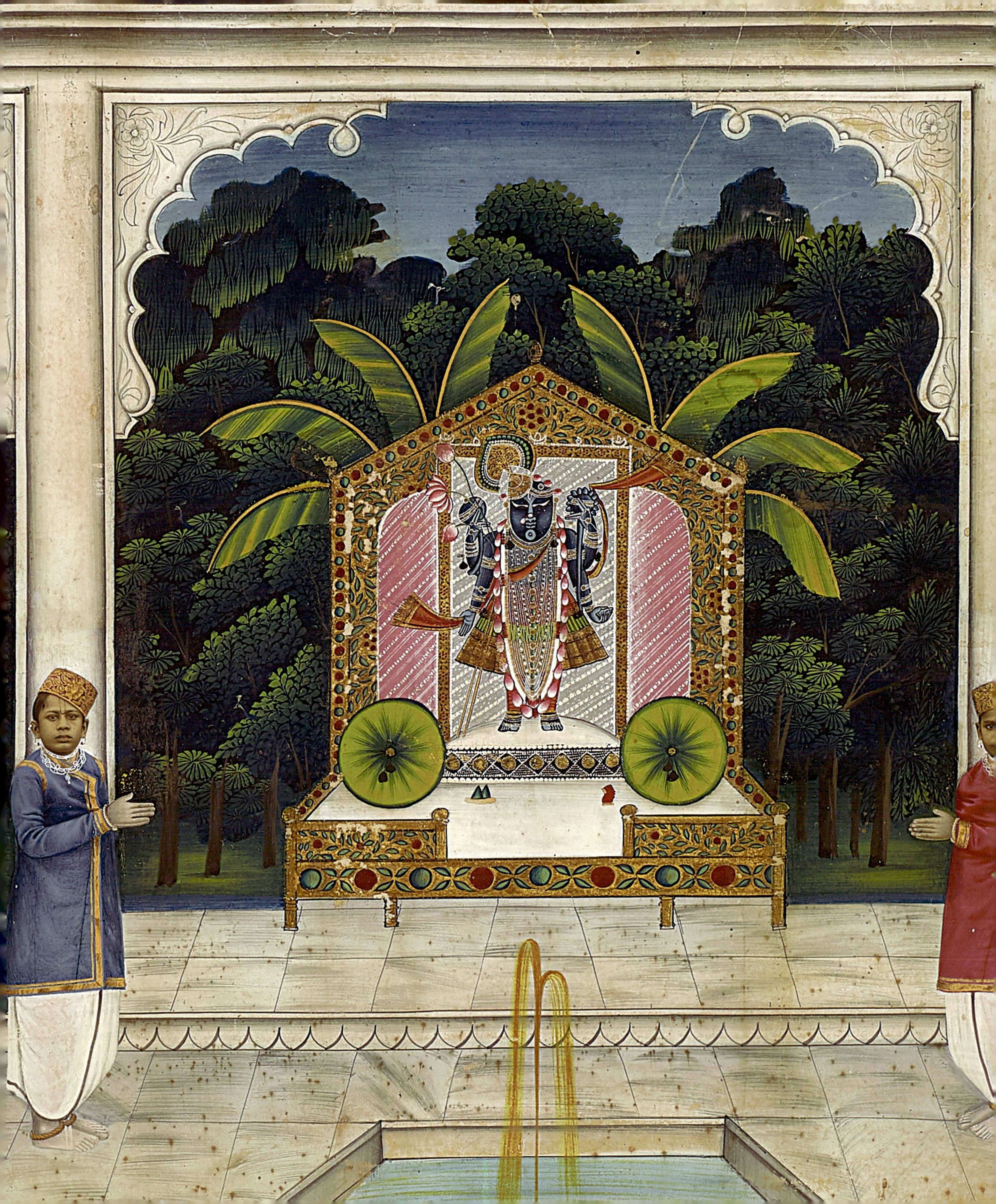

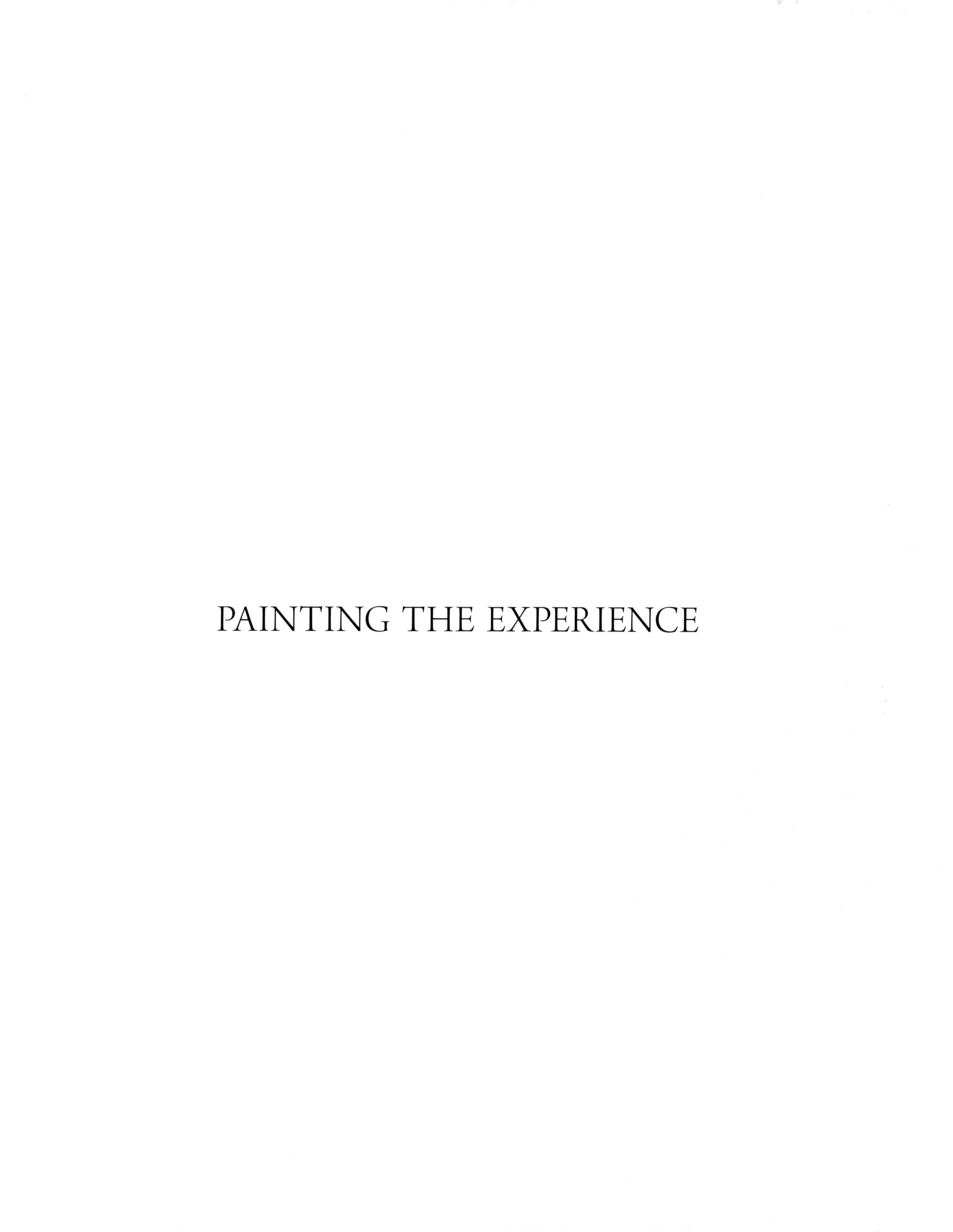

PAINTING THE EXPERIENCE

Framing the analysis

The following sections subdivide popular *manoraths* into three main processes of execution: miniature painting, mixed-media, and photography. There will be important digressions: on iconography, exploring liturgical depictions and their meanings; on style, covering such topics as the adoption of the miniature painting mode in conjunction with a photo-realistic vocabulary on a single picture plane; and on issues of technique and terminology, making a clear distinction between mixed-media painting and painted photography. There are also specific sections describing ways of customizing the *manoraths* according to the commissioners' tastes; tackling compositional issues, such as the use of temple backgrounds or idyllic landscapes; and defining Khubiram and Gopilal studio's practices.

This investigation is based on a careful analysis of popular *manoraths* in the collection of Anil Relia. A close examination reveals some surprising details: only a small number of images can be defined as traditional miniature paintings, whereas most of the works were executed using a mixed-media technique. The collection also includes *manoraths* in other media: two are painted photographs and three are gelatin silver prints. While these proportions suggest that the mixed-media technique was the most common process of execution, we must refrain from drawing conclusions based on a single archive. Instead, we can take advantage of this investigation to reflect on the different processes of execution and to propose a more nuanced reading of these techniques. This critical issue, not fully explored in previous studies, will reveal some other unanticipated details.

Painted *manoraths*: staging an experience of the mind

Among the examples of early *manoraths* in the collection, there are five works executed using the traditional miniature painting technique (Cat. nos. 1–5). The earliest of them, dated to c. 1900–1910, is Cat. no. 1, a painting executed by the renowned artist Ghasiram (Ghasiram Hardev Sharma, 1868–1930), whose name appears on the back of the work.[29] Its central tableau displays a compositional scheme typical of many *manorath* paintings: in the inner sanctum, Tilkayat Govardhanlal, holding an *arati* lamp, is standing next to Shrinathji. The inner sanctum is the most sacred space of the Nathdwara temple, which, as a protection against ritual pollution, is only accessible to the sect's priests and a handful of individuals working for the temple. The adjoining grey room, depicted in Cat. no. 1 and many other *manoraths*, is the area where the public stands when taking *darshan* of Shrinathji. Pilgrims would enter from a door on the left, take *darshan*, and leave through a doorway on the right, which leads to one of the many courtyards of the *haveli* temple. Such ritual viewing is possible only at specific times of the day.

Three other miniature paintings display similar compositional traits. Cat. no. 2 depicts a couple next to the shrine of Shrinathji and, in the sanctum, Govardhanlal with an unidentified priest. The work is inscribed with the name of the artist, Raghunath Sukhdev (also Rugnath Sukhdev, 1882–1924), and it can be dated to c. 1910. Cat. no. 3 represents a family of five and, in the inner sanctum of the temple, both Govardhanlal and his son Damodarlal. The painting can be dated about 1920 on the basis of the portrayal of the two priests. The work bears an inscription indicating that Ambalal Khemraj executed this work.[30] Cat. no. 4 depicts a numerous family of pilgrims from Jamnagar, Gujarat, standing in the grey antechamber adjoining the inner sanctum. It is dated *samvat* 1977 (1920 CE) and bears an inscription with the name of the painter, Nathalal Jaikrishnadas. A horizontal format was deployed in

29. For another *manorath* painted by Ghasiram, see Ambalal, *Krishna as Shrinathji* 90. The same artist also worked in the mixed-media technique, as in Cat. no. 7. For his life and works, see Lyons 168–202.

30. Ambalal Khemraj was also a photographer. Circa 1920 he took an important photograph documenting the artists in his clan. This image is published as the frontispiece of Lyons's book.

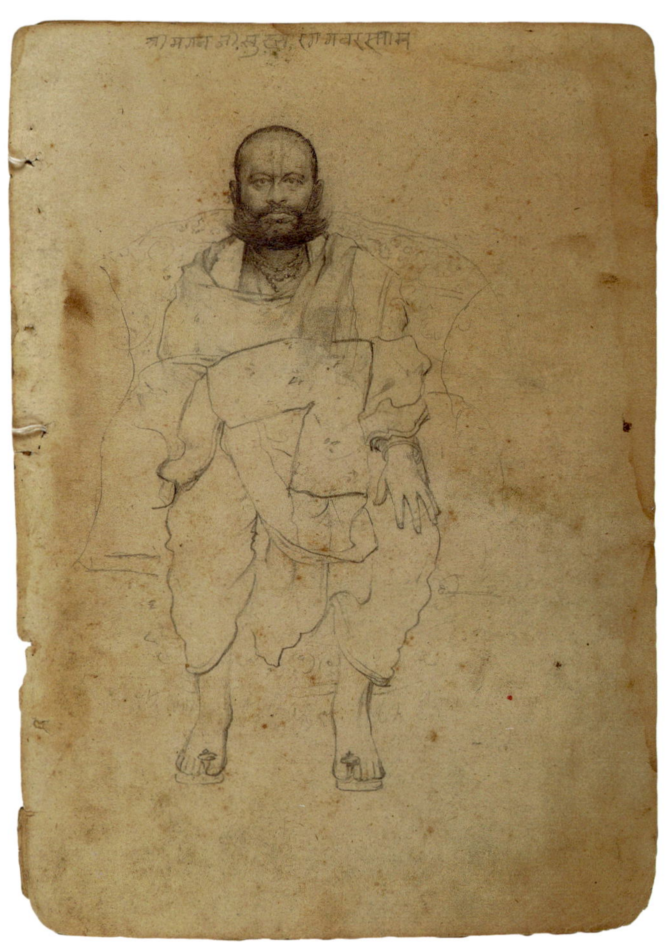

FIGURE 5.

Preliminary Study of Maganlal's Portrait.

Page from a sketchbook; pencil on paper; c. 1900. 9.5 x 6.7 in. (24.1 x 17 cm).

this case to accommodate the large group of devotees. Inside the shrine are, once again, Govardhanlal holding the *arati* lamp and Damodarlal holding a peacock fan. The two priests are indeed ubiquitous figures in *manorath* painting, indicating their popularity and the reverential esteem in which they were held.

Such liturgical depictions suggest that a private *darshan* to Shrinathji is taking place in the Nathdwara temple. The pilgrims are portrayed as if they were standing in adoration in the adjoining room. However, this is something that would not be feasible in real life; in fact, the temple tends to be very crowded during the daily *darshan*s, and it would be impossible for any devotee to have such a close encounter or a private viewing with the head priest and the icon. In this respect, *manorath*s are constructed images about the experience of being at Nathdwara on pilgrimage rather than faithful depictions of actual events.

Cat. no. 5 was painted by the famous Nathdwara artist Champalal Hiralal Gaur (c. 1875–1930) many of whose other works are known, including *Mantubai's Manorath of Sanjhi* (Fig. 4).[31] While this work follows the same compositional arrangement seen in the *manorath*s above, it differs in the depiction of the priests in the inner sanctum, revealing the devotees' affiliation with the temple of Balkrishnaji of Surat. The priest on the left can be identified as Goswami Maganlal of Surat (1840–1897), as confirmed by two preparatory drawings of the same subject, one in the collection of Anil Relia (Fig. 5) and the other in Champalal's sketchbook.[32] The priest standing across from him is Vrajratanlal (1896–1992), Maganlal's son, who became the *goswami* of Surat as an infant, after his father's death. His mature likeness provides important clues to date this anachronistic work to the mid-1920s. Champalal's mastery and interest in portraiture can be further appreciated in a preliminary drawing of the two devotees, whose sketches were made in preparation for this *manorath* (Fig. 6).[33]

31. For the life and work of Champalal, see Lyons 101–126.

32. See Lyons, fig. 94.

33. For another preparatory sketch, by the same artist, also to be used in a *manorath*, see Lyons, fig. 92.

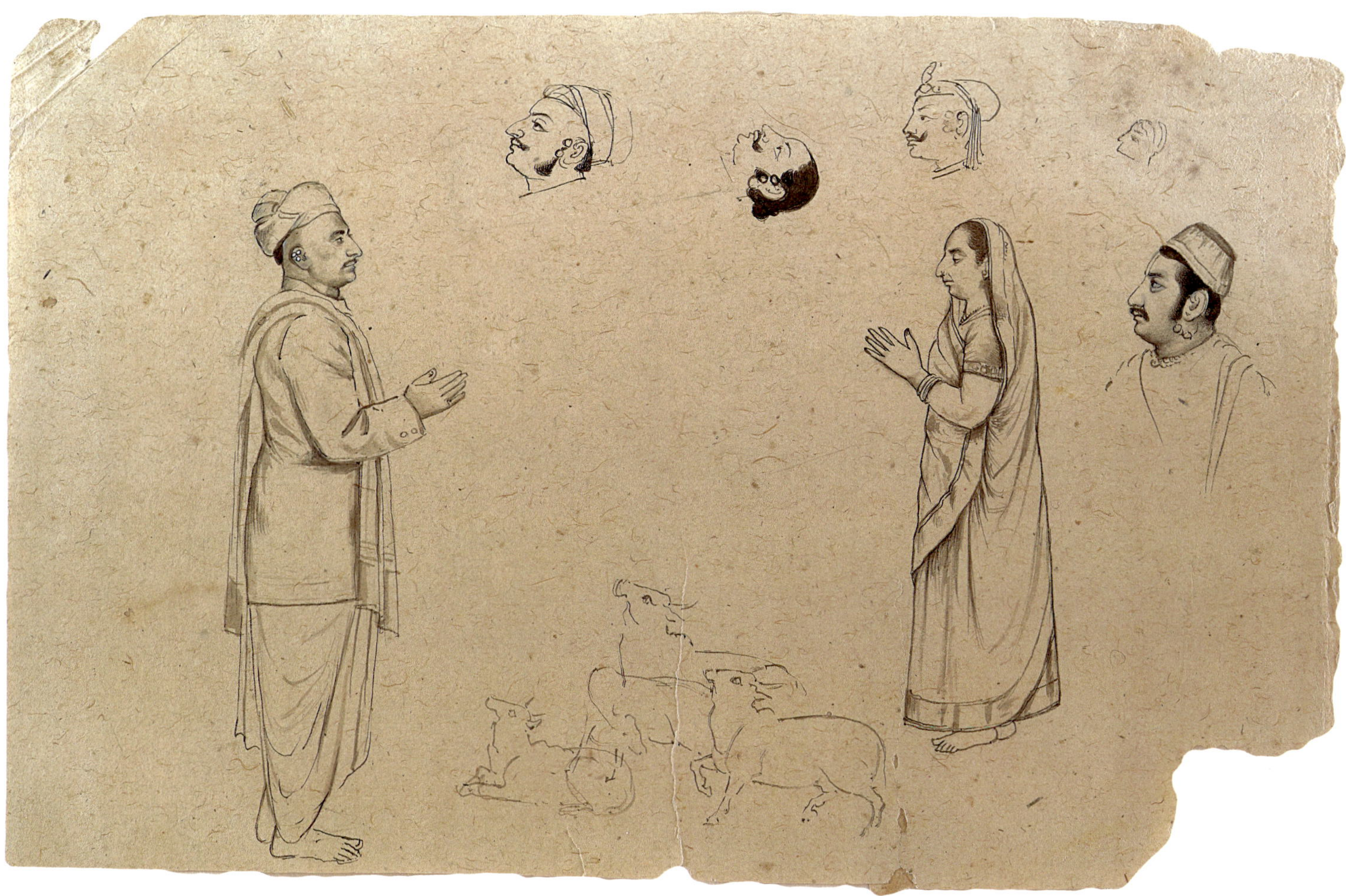

FIGURE 6.
Preliminary Drawing of Two Devotees and Other Portraits.
By Champalal Hiralal Gaur;
ink and pencil on paper; c. mid-1920s.
9.1 x 13.8 in. (23 x 35 cm).

Nathdwara miniature painting and the photo-realistic style

One of the distinctive features of painted *manoraths* (as in Cat. nos. 1–4) is the adoption of two different visual vocabularies for the portrayal of the human figures: a traditional one, from Nathdwara miniature painting, for the representation of the priests, and a photo-realistic one for the worshippers. This stylistic juxtaposition needs to be contextualized. Paintings reproducing photographic conventions—such as the photo-realistic treatment of a sitter's face or the arrangement of a composition in imitation of studio backdrops—were very much in vogue at the time of Govardhanlal, and this is when they started to be used alongside the Nathdwara miniature painting style. Very far from being a local phenomenon, this interest in photographic conventions also emerged in Rajput court painting around the 1870s.[34]

34. See Aitken; and Dewan, "A Tale of Two Mediums."

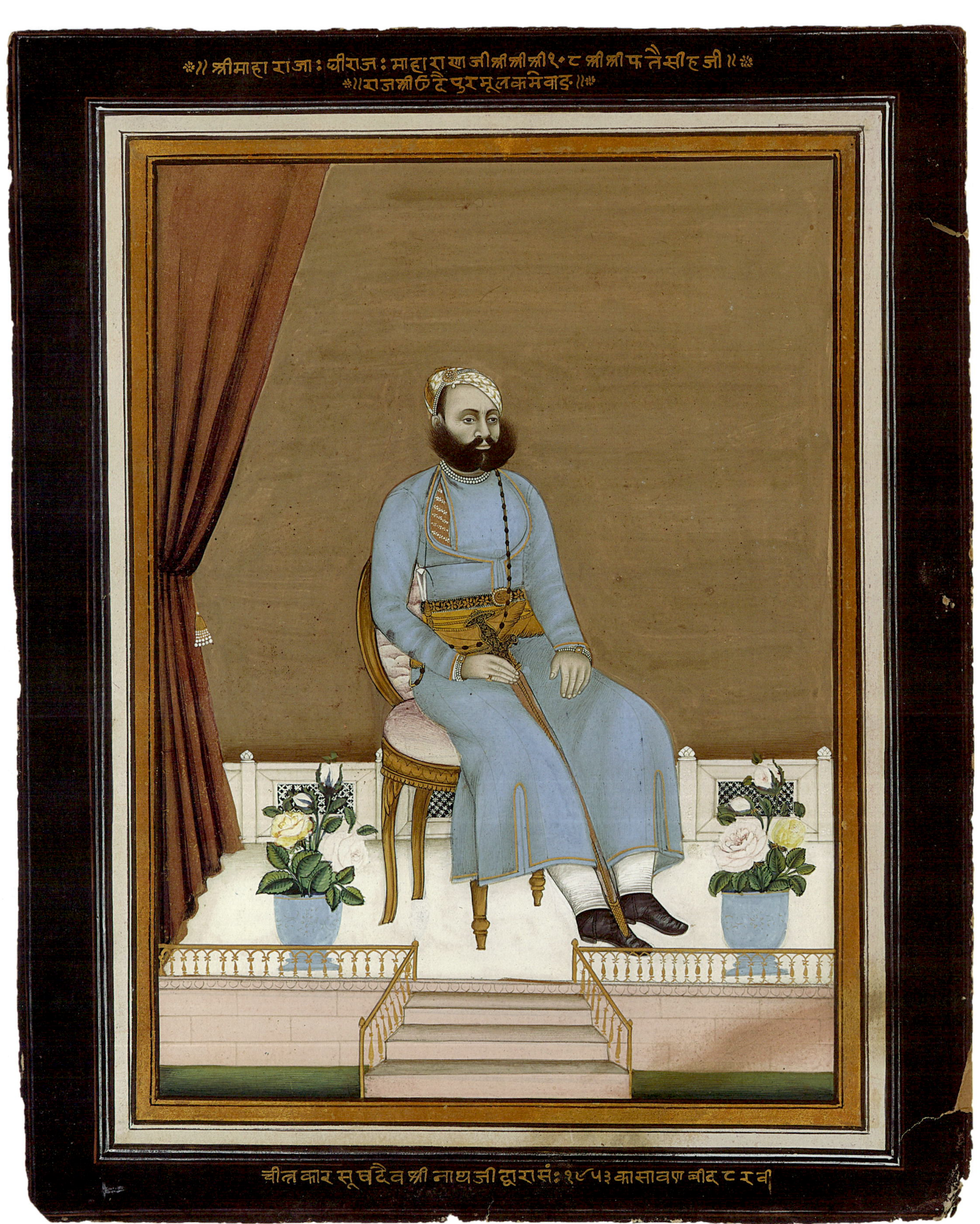
॥ श्रीमाहाराजाधीराज माहाराणाजी श्री श्री श्री १०८ श्री श्री फतैसीहजी ॥
॥ राज श्री उदैपुर मूलक मेवाड़ ॥
चीत्तकार सूखदेव श्री नाथजी दूरा सं: १९५३ का सावण बीद ८ रवी

FIGURE 7A.

Portrait of Maharana Fateh Singh of Mewar.
By Sukhdev Kishandas;
opaque watercolour and gold on paper; dated samvat 1953 (1896 CE).
12.2 x 9.8 in. (31 x 25 cm).

FIGURE 7B.

Portrait of Maharana Fateh Singh of Mewar.
Detail of Fig. 7a.

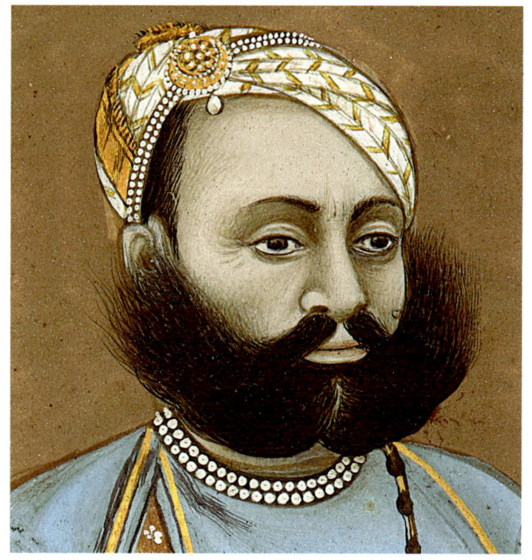

An example of a Nathdwara miniature painting that selectively adopts both stylistic and compositional features from photography is the portrait of Maharana Fateh Singh of Mewar (r. 1884–1930) (Fig. 7a). This work, dated *samvat* 1953 (1896 CE), was executed by Sukhdev Kishandas (1853–1925), the director *(mukhiya)* of the painting department of the Shrinathji temple.[35] For the portrayal of the sitter, the artist employed a photographic treatment of his face in which, with purely pictorial means, he imitated the sepia monochrome tonalities of a photograph (Fig. 7b). Also, its compositional arrangement is reminiscent of the conventions of studio photographs, as, for example, in the pose of the sitter and in the use of props, such as the flower vases and the draped curtain. The artist did not, however, intend to imitate a painted photograph; rather, he selectively incorporated certain visual devices from this medium to modernize his work. This painting exemplifies one of the numerous ways in which painters adapted photographic conventions, which had become an integral part of the Nathdwara pictorial repertoire by the late nineteenth century. These conventions were used in different degrees and combinations: for example, the *manorath* paintings above incorporate a photo-realistic treatment of the devotees but rely on the traditional schemes of Nathdwara painting for the background and composition.

In *manoraths*, the optical play between the miniature painting style and the photo-realistic mode of representation are used in a meaningful way: they suggest a spatiotemporal subdivision between transcendental and worldly domains. In particular, the heavy shading of the photo-realistic style provides the devotees with a tangible aura which places them in the terrestrial domain. By contrast, the idealized miniature painting technique used for the priests standing in the inner sanctum situates them in a transcendental realm. This same visual play can be seen in a memorial portrait of a Pushti Marg priest in the collection (Fig. 8a).

35. This painting is also discussed in Nardi, "*Manorath* of Śrī Nāthjī."

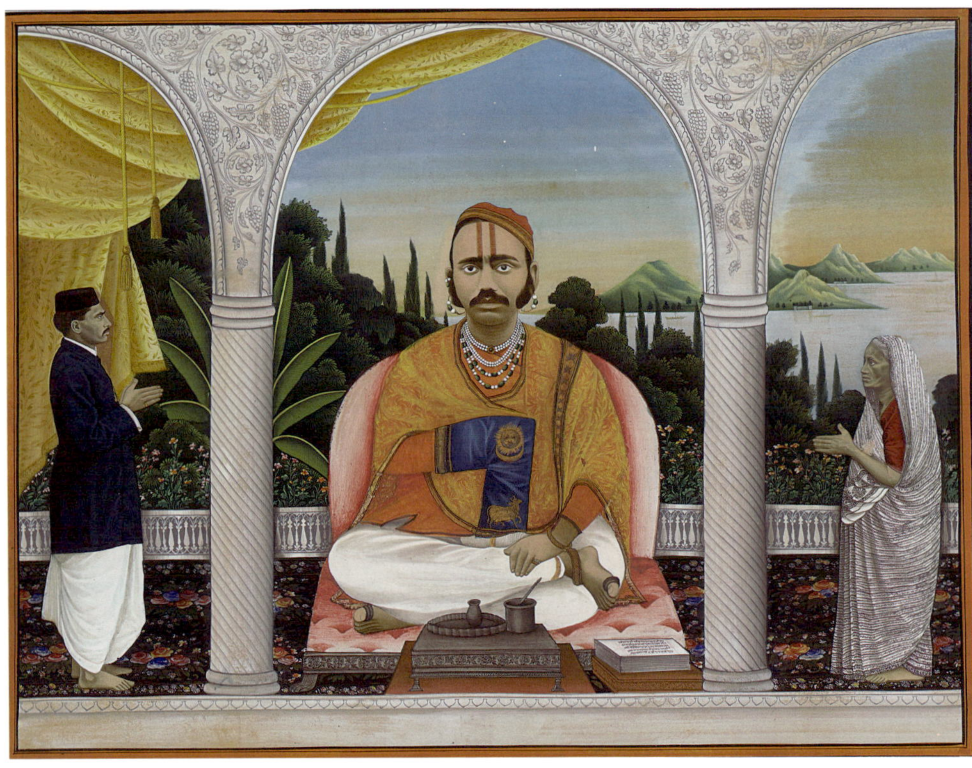

FIGURE 8A.
Memorial Portrait of Goswami Kanhaiyalal of Mathura.
Inscribed to Khubiram Sharma, attributed to Raghunath Sukhdev;
opaque watercolour and gold on paper; c. 1911.
20.1 x 25.2 in. (51.1 x 64 cm).

Memorial portraits, another common genre of Nathdwara painting, were commissioned to commemorate deceased people, such as priests or family members.[36] Fig. 8a depicts Goswami Kanhaiyalal of Mathura (1868–1911), a religious personality known to be a patron of music and literature. The work, inscribed with the name Khubiram Sharma, can be dated to c. 1911, the year in which the priest died. His figure, noticeably bigger than those of the devotees, was based on a photographic model as suggested by his iconic pose, reiterated in pictorial form in this and other paintings.[37] Even though his likeness was based on a photograph, his face does not display a photo-realistic style, but rather an idealized countenance intensified by his *darshanik* frontal view. This treatment stands in sharp contrast to that of the devotees, who are depicted with dense photo-realistic features. In particular, the woman on the right displays exaggerated skin folds and sunken cheeks (Fig. 8b). The pronounced difference between the two styles suggests, again, the distinction between the transcendental and the worldly domains—a divergence that is further intensified by the subdivision of space. The three figures stand on a terrace divided into three distinctive areas by an arched colonnade, which highlights the centrality of the priest and suggests hierarchy. This partition of space is comparable to that of *manorath* paintings in

36. For a mixed-media *manorath* that was conceived as a memorial portrait, see Dewan, *Embellished Reality*, cat. no. 24. As Dewan explains, the blurry quality of the portrait suggests that the likeness of the sitter was "extracted from another photograph," meaning that a family member of the devotee must have brought a photograph to Nathdwara to commission the work. This memorial portrait was meant to celebrate the devotee's lifelong allegiance to Pushti Marg.

37. For a painting similar in subject, style, and composition, see Ruia, fig. 4. This painting is inscribed with the name of Raghunath Sukhdev. The visual correspondence between Ruia's painting and Fig. 8a casts some doubt on Khubiram's authorship of the latter. For this reason, we have attributed it to Raghunath. This ascription is justified by the questionable practices of the Khubiram and Gopilal workshop which, often, did not recognize professional painters' authorship, instead placing their own names on the finished works. This topic is further elaborated below.

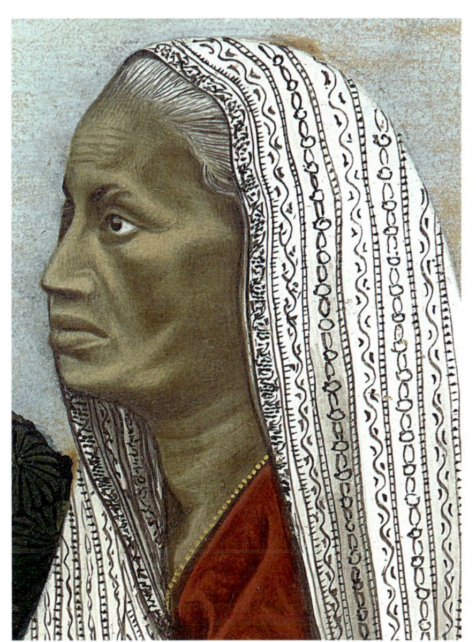

FIGURE 8B.
Portrait of a Woman.
Detail of Fig. 8a.

which the priests and Shrinathji appear in the sanctum of the Nathdwara temple and the devotees stand in the nearby antechamber.

Mixed-media *manoraths*: between painting and photography

The vast majority of works in the collection are executed in a mixed-media technique (Cat. nos. 6–30). The principal difference between the painted *manoraths* and their mixed-media counterparts is in the way they achieve the photo-realistic style used to represent the devotees. The mixed-media works adopted a semi-mechanical method of execution, pasting a black-and-white print of the faces or busts of the devotees onto the surface of the painting. This simplified process developed in response to an increased number of pilgrims commissioning *manorath* images and requiring them to be finished in the shortest time possible—that is, during the course of the pilgrimage trip itself. It was unquestionably easier to take their photograph in a studio than to have their portraits painted by professional artists.

Our analysis suggests that there were at least two distinct, yet comparable, techniques for executing these mixed-media *manoraths*. One process consisted in pasting to the paper surface cut-outs of black-and-white photographs of the devotees' faces. The edges of the cut-outs were subsequently covered with a layer of opaque watercolour. This procedure was used for Cat. nos. 6 and 10. In Cat. no. 10, the thickness and some creasing of the two affixed prints remain visible, as shown in Fig. 9, whereas in Cat. no. 6 they are skillfully camouflaged. Fig. 10 shows how the artist, Udairam Bhagvandas, succeeded in disguising the edges and thickness of the photograph with a substantial layer of pigments and by adding flowers around the head of the devotees. This solution makes the presence of the print noticeable only on close inspection.[38] An unfinished portrait of Govardhanlal (Fig. 11) reveals this process of execution. A cut-out photograph of the bust of the priest is glued to the surface of the painting, and a sketch in black ink delineates his figure sitting in an interior.

This technique poses a question of terminology, as it may be tempting to classify it as collage. However, a close comparison of mixed-media *manoraths* and collages—both popular at the time—reveals that the two techniques have divergent visual objectives,

38. This image is analyzed in Nardi, "*Manorath* of Śrī Nāthjī."

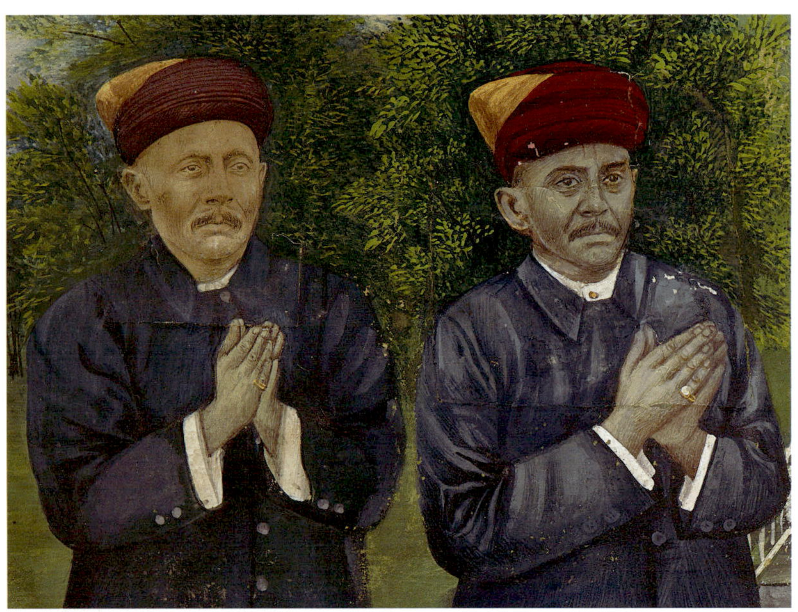

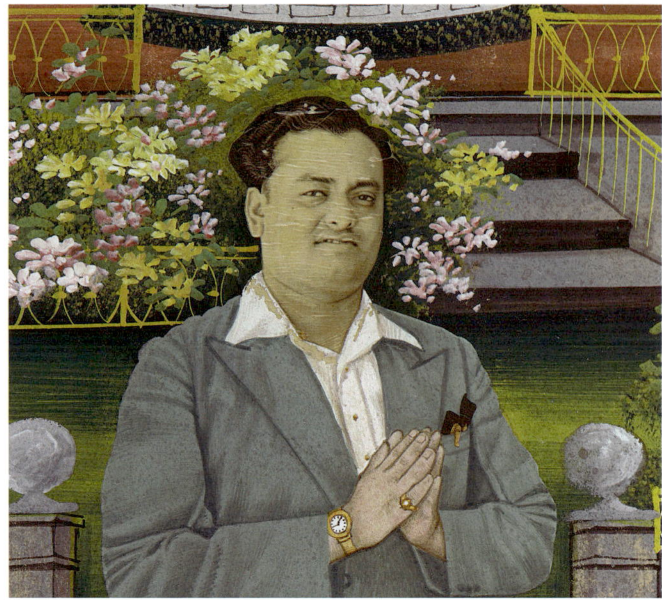

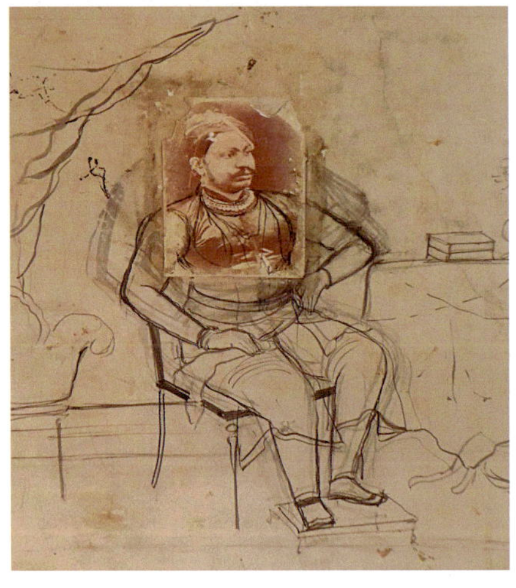

FIGURE 9.
Portrait of Two Devotees.
Detail of Cat. no. 10.

Figure 10.
Portrait of a Devotee.
Detail of Cat. no. 6.

FIGURE 11.
Unfinished Portrait of Govardhanlal.
Cut-and-pasted gelatin silver print and ink on paper; c. 1920.
19.5 x 25 in. (49.5 x 63.5 cm).
Courtesy of Aditya Ruia.

which impact their final optical results. In the two *manorath*s above (Cat. nos. 6, 10), the black-and-white cut-out prints served as aids to reproduce accurate likenesses of the devotees and to achieve the desired photo-realistic style, which had already been popularized by earlier miniature paintings (e.g., Fig. 7b). The fact that the artists concealed the textural differences of the two media by covering the edges of the print and by painting on top of the photograph makes such works dissimilar from collages in which heterogeneous media are juxtaposed so as to draw attention to their differences. A good example of a collage is Fig. 12, a work produced in Nathdwara in the 1930s. It is clear that the silhouettes of Krishna and the *gopi*s are cut-outs of popular prints pasted on a painted surface representing the idyllic landscape of Braj. A collage such as Fig. 12 is made with the intention of emphasizing the textural dissimilarities of the painted surface and the print.[39]

The second method of producing mixed-media *manorath*s is much more difficult to detect with the naked eye. Like the previous one, this process also entailed extracting the faces or busts of the devotees from photographs. Before pasting the cut-outs on the works, however, the cut-outs were rendered very thin by removing the unnecessary layers of paper from their backs until they became translucent, like onionskins. Once pasted and painted over, they were undetectable to the naked eye.

39. For similar collages, see J. Jain, cat. nos. VII.6, VII.26, VII.28, VII.24. For an introduction to collages which adopt landscapes painted in Nathdwara, see J. Jain 78–79 and passim.

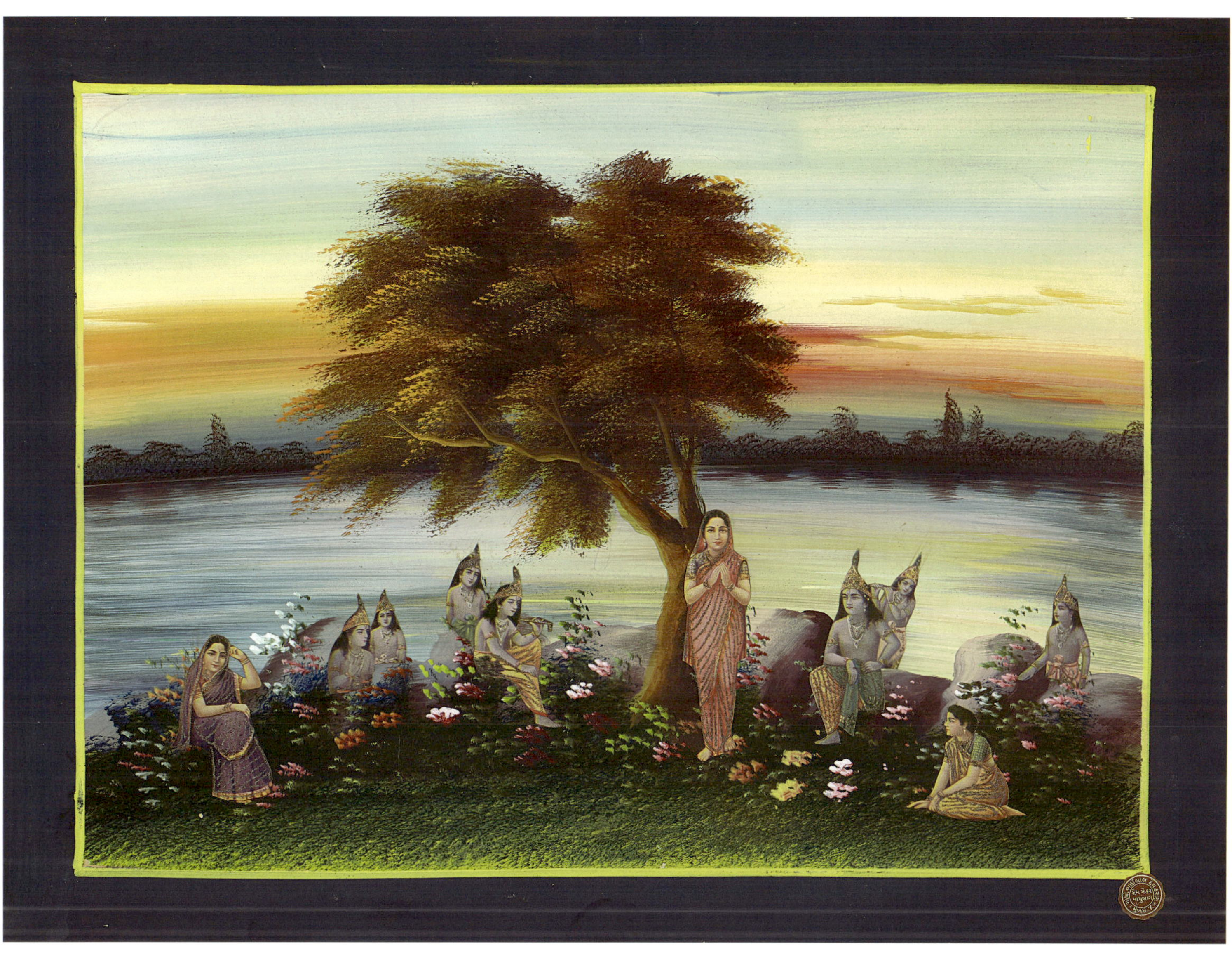

FIGURE 12.

Krishna and the *Gopis* in a Landscape.

Collage; c. 1930s.
17.9 x 24 in. (45.5 x 61 cm).

This process is explained by Kajri Jain: "The photographs, printed on special imported matt paper (which enabled overpainting), would have much of their backing scraped away to make them as thin as possible before they were carefully pasted in place and overpainted to merge with the rest of the painting."[40] This technique was adopted in the execution of Fig. 13a. This unfinished memorial portrait is extremely valuable in understanding the technique of execution. In the close-up (Fig. 13b) one can hardly see the physiognomic traits of the sitter. Though barely perceptible, they were just visible enough for a painter to enhance them with colour, so retaining the likeness of

40. See K. Jain 382–383 n. 12. The same technical process is also explained in Ruia 69.

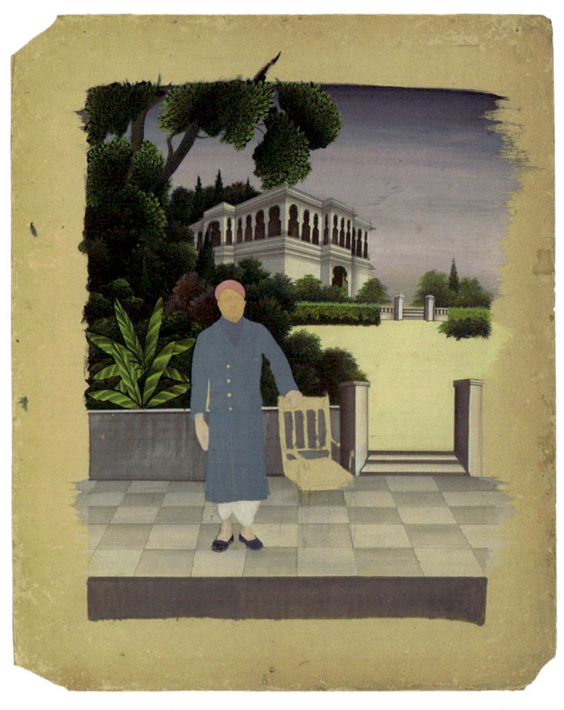

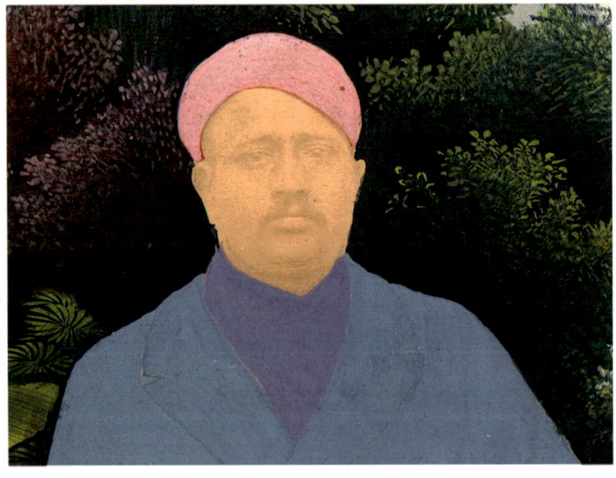

FIGURE 13A.

Unfinished Memorial Portrait.

Cut-and-pasted gelatin silver print, opaque watercolour on paper; c. 1930s–1940s. 25.2 x 20.1 in (64 x 51.1 cm).

FIGURE 13B.

Unfinished Portrait of a Man.

Detail of Fig. 13a.

the devotee.[41] Because of this technology, many mixed-media *manorath*s have been confounded with painted photographs, with which they share stylistic similarities. This issue is further elaborated below.

The uncovering of this second process answers a crucial terminological question. While some pioneering studies on Indian photography have categorized mixed-media *manorath*s as painted photographs, this classification does not fit the works under examination here.[42] Mixed-media *manorath*s, as for example Cat. no. 21, do resemble painted photographs but, technically speaking, they are not. A closer look at Cat. no. 21 shows that the garments and feet of the devotees were first drawn and then painted over (Fig. 14), and we can assume that the entire composition was painted in the same way. The small yet significant presence of cut-out photographs of their faces, which remain invisible in the finished works, is not sufficient to categorize these images as painted photographs. Hence, the present study proposes to make a clear differentiation between painted photography and mixed-media painting: while the mixed-media category defines works that are painted and use cut-out photographs for the portraits, the painted photography classification indicates that a black-and-white print has been painted over (Cat. no. 31) or lightly tinted (Cat. no. 34). Such terminological distinction reflects a more precise definition of technique and it better elucidates the flexible boundaries between photography and painting.

Customizing the composition

An interesting piece of evidence on the process of assembling mixed-media *manorath*s is provided by a devotee who visited the temple with her family at a young age—the girl wearing a pink sari in Cat. no. 28. In a

41. This technique can also be seen in an unfinished portrait of Govardhanlal in the collection of Aditya Ruia (Ruia, fig. 39), in which a thin print with uneven edges representing the priest is glued to a paper surface using a white paste.

42. Two sources that have considered such *manorath*s as painted photographs are Allana and Kumar; and Dewan, *Embellished Reality*. My intention is not to criticize these authors, whose works are of such great importance in the study of photography in India. Rather, this finding strengthens their views on the diverse modalities in which the photographic medium has been appropriated in the Indian context.

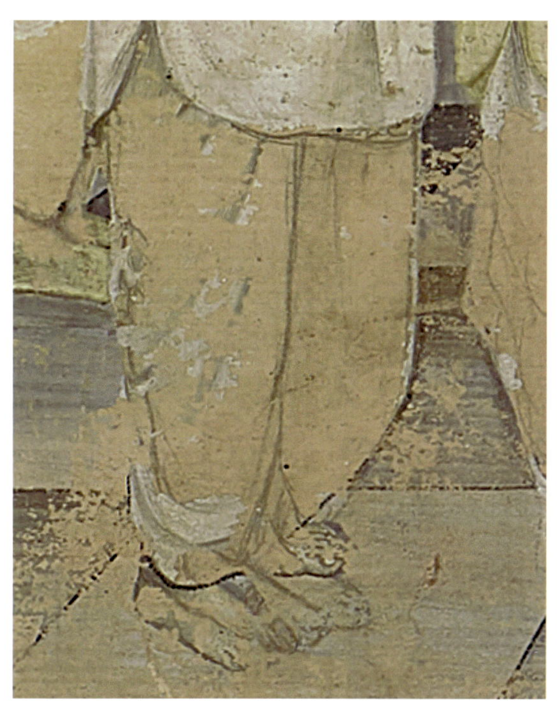

FIGURE 14.
Underdrawings.
Detail of Cat. no. 21.

recent interview conducted by Anil Relia, this devotee claims to have gone on a trip from her hometown of Ahmedabad to Nathdwara in c. 1946.[43] She remembers going to an art studio where an artist accompanied the family upstairs and took photographs of them, separately, posing against a plain cloth. This valuable information substantiates that photographs were taken individually and not in groups. The photographs were subsequently developed, cut, thinned, and arranged on a painted surface according to gender distinction and hierarchy.

After the photographs were taken, devotees would have also been given the opportunity to decide certain details regarding their outfits and backgrounds. An interesting example of the types of customization can be seen by comparing two *manorath*s, representing two sisters, executed by Bhuralal Motilalnath Sharma (b. 1899) in the 1930s or 1940s.[44] Fig. 15 and Cat. no. 19 portray the women in what seems, at a first look, an identical composition. A closer analysis, however, reveals some important differences in the designs of their saris and in the *pichhwai*s hanging behind the icon of Shrinathji. The two *manorath*s indicate that while the photographs of the sisters were taken only once, the two commissioners made different choices about how their outfits and backgrounds would appear in the finished works.

In terms of backdrops, a close analysis of the collection reveals that a substantial number of pilgrims chose to be depicted while celebrating Gopashtami, the festival of cattle. Many images, in fact, depict this occasion, which is indicated by the sanctum being decorated with a *pichhwai* representing cows placed behind Shrinathji (Cat. nos. 3–5, 18–24, 28–29). This doesn't necessarily mean that the pilgrims visited the temple during Gopashtami. Rather, it indicates that this iconography was a favorite stock theme.

Cat. no. 8 further strengthens the assumption that backgrounds were not used to place the pilgrims in the spatiotemporal frameworks of their actual visits. This work, executed by Kanhaiyalal Bhimraj, depicts four devotees standing in the Shrinathji temple while a special celebration is being performed. In the inner sanctum, there

43. Personal communication with Anil Relia, August 2018.

44. The name Bhuralal Motilalnath Sharma is inscribed only on Fig. 15. For five memorial portraits by the same artist, see Agarvwal 108–109.

FIGURE 15.
***Manorath* with Two Sisters.**
By Bhuralal Motilalnath;
cut-and-pasted gelatin silver prints, opaque watercolour and gold on paper;
c. 1930s–1940s.
25 x 20 in. (63.5 x 51 cm).
Courtesy of Vivek Nanda.

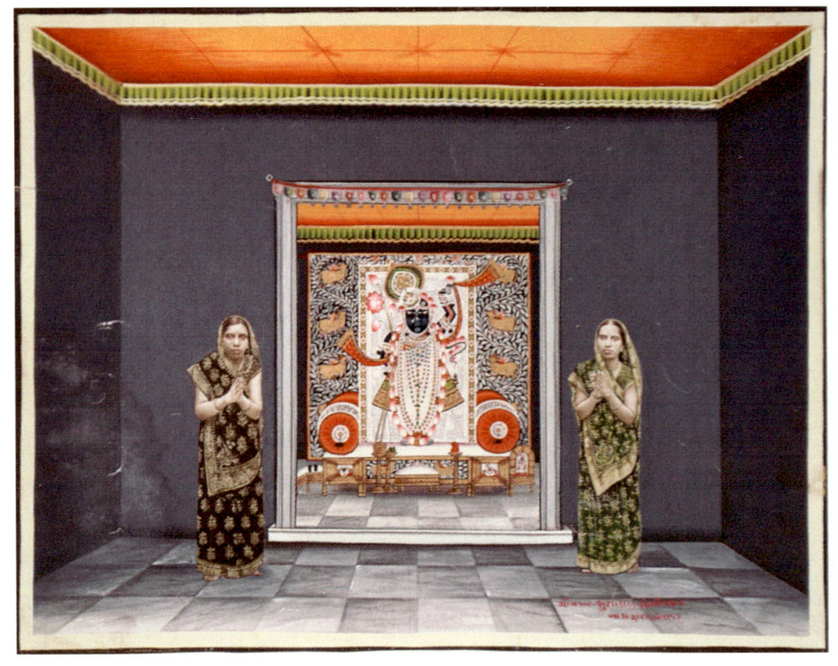

is an assembly of four icons: Shrinathji and Navnitpriyaji in the centre, Mathureshji of Kota on the left and Dvarkadishji of Kankroli on the right. Standing on the right is a priest who can be identified as Goswami Ranchhorlal (born 1851), the custodian of Mathureshji. The priest brought this important Pushti Marg icon to Nathdwara in 1908 for the celebration of a series of liturgical performances which took place in conjunction with the Festival of the Five *Svarups* (Fig. 3). The date of execution of Cat. no. 8, however, is subsequent to the celebrations: it can be assigned to the mid-1920s. The selection of that specific occasion as a backdrop suggests the aspiration of the commissioner to be staged in an auspicious moment in the liturgical history of the temple. The work also indicates his personal affiliation with the Pushti Marg temple of Kota. Such anachronistic depictions were frequent. Other examples are Cat. no. 5, analyzed above, and Cat. no. 25, a work dated 1941 which portrays Govardhanlal, who died in 1934. In this case the commissioner wanted to celebrate his special connection with this esteemed figure.

Staging the garden of Krishna

A number of *manoraths* in the collection (Cat. nos. 6–7, 9–14, 20) are set in gardens. These are executed in the mixed-media technique, and their visual vocabulary combines the photo-realistic treatment of the devotees, the Nathdwara miniature painting style for the representation of familiar figures (e.g., Shrinathji and Govardhanlal), and idealized backgrounds in bold colours which engage with western academicism. This melding creates great visual tension on the surface of the works.

The backgrounds of these works provide greater chromatic richness and visual variety than what we see in the *manorath*s staged inside the temple. The gardens include palatial mansions, distant landscapes, and multiple vanishing points in a combination of spatiotemporal layers that evokes the imaginary idyll of Braj. This configuration can be interpreted as a vernacular version of Victorian pastoral landscapes. Such backgrounds were not exclusive to *manorath* images; they were recurrent also in other genres, such as representations of Krishna and memorial portraits (Fig. 8a). As explained by Ambalal, this scenery, introduced in Nathdwara painting at the end of the nineteenth century, was considered particularly suitable for the representation of mythological themes.[45] Followers of Pushti Marg associated the picturesque bodies of water with the Yamuna river and the lush vegetation with Vrindavan, the locale of the *lila*s of Krishna. Concurrently, these constructed mythic territories were also imbued with overtones that connected them with Nathdwara. The depiction of devotees near sumptuous mansions (Cat. nos. 6–7, 9) evoked their physical proximity to the *haveli* temple of Shrinathji, which is styled as a royal palace. This codified visual language was intelligible to Pushti Marg audiences, as it related with the affective sphere of their devotional experience.

The *manorath*s in the collection that are set in these timeless garden landscapes display different levels of artistic skill: some of them exhibit complex configurations whereas others repeat a recurrent formula. Among the more elaborate images are Cat. nos. 6–7 and 9, which are noticeably intricate and would have required considerable time and inventiveness to execute. Cat. no. 7 is inscribed with the name of Ghasiram (1868–1930), one of the most popular Nathdwara artists at the time. He is known to have left his hometown in 1918 to work for a few years at the court of Jhalawar, in southern Rajasthan. Cat. no. 7 may be dated to 1925–1930, after his return to Nathdwara, a period that coincides with the booming of the *manorath* genre.[46]

The more simplified versions of *manorath*s set in gardens suggest a semi-mechanical mode of reproduction. For example, Cat. nos. 10–11 and 14 share a number of

45. See Ambalal, *Krishna as Shrinathji* 82.

46. For Ghasiram's stay at the court of Jhalawar, see Nardi, "Portraiture and Politics."

compositional features, such as the icon of Shrinathji standing in a white marble pavilion, or *bangla*, with a palatial mansion on the right. Cat. no. 11 bears an obliterated inscription which can be reconstructed as spelling "Khubiram and Gopilal." This inscription indicates that the work was prepared by multiple collaborators of the Khubiram and Gopilal studio. The practice of this workshop is discussed below.

Khubiram and Gopilal: the studio as a brand name

Many of the more formulaic *manoraths* in the collection bear inscriptions mentioning two names, Khubiram and Gopilal. These are written in a variety of handwritings and scripts (usually Hindi and Gujarati, but sometimes English). The names are inscribed in slightly different forms, such as *Chitrakar Khubiram Gopilal* (Cat. nos. 24–25), *Chitrakar Khubiram Gopilal Sharma* (Cat. nos. 17, 31; Fig. 16), and *Chitrakar Khubiram Bhai Gopilal* (Cat. nos. 14–16, 21–23). The variations in nomenclature are not limited to the examples above, and, as we shall see, they do not point to authorship but to this workshop as a "brand name."[47]

The two names belong to two trained painters, the partners Khubiram Nathuji Sharma (1880-1966) and Gopilal Govardhanlal Sharma (1890–1970). Some information on these two individuals was gathered by Anil Relia in 2018, when he had the opportunity to interview some of their family members in Nathdwara.[48] They recounted that Khubiram had moved from Udaipur to Nathdwara at the age of ten, after he had had an accident in a stone mine where he was working. This was when he started selling, on the streets of Nathdwara, some of the artworks made by his mother from whom he learned the art of painting. Very early in his life he met Gopilal and started selling his works as well. In 1907, they started a partnership which lasted for many years. Later in his life, he operated his own studio, the Artist Khubiram and Sons, which he handed down to his sons and is still active today (Fig. 2b; Cat. no. 30).[49]

47. The expression "brand name" is adopted from K. Jain 206–207, where it is used in the context of Indian popular prints.

48. Personal communication with Anil Relia, August 2018.

49. For Khubiram and the Artist Khubiram and Sons studio, see Pinney, *Photos of the Gods* 157–158. Pinney observes that paintings inscribed to Artist Khubiram and Sons, which appear from the 1940s, indicate "a co-operative effort between Khubiram and one or more of his six sons, all of whom were artists." While the precise date in which this studio superseded the Khubiram and Gopilal workshop remains unknown, dated works suggest that this succession took place around the late 1940s.

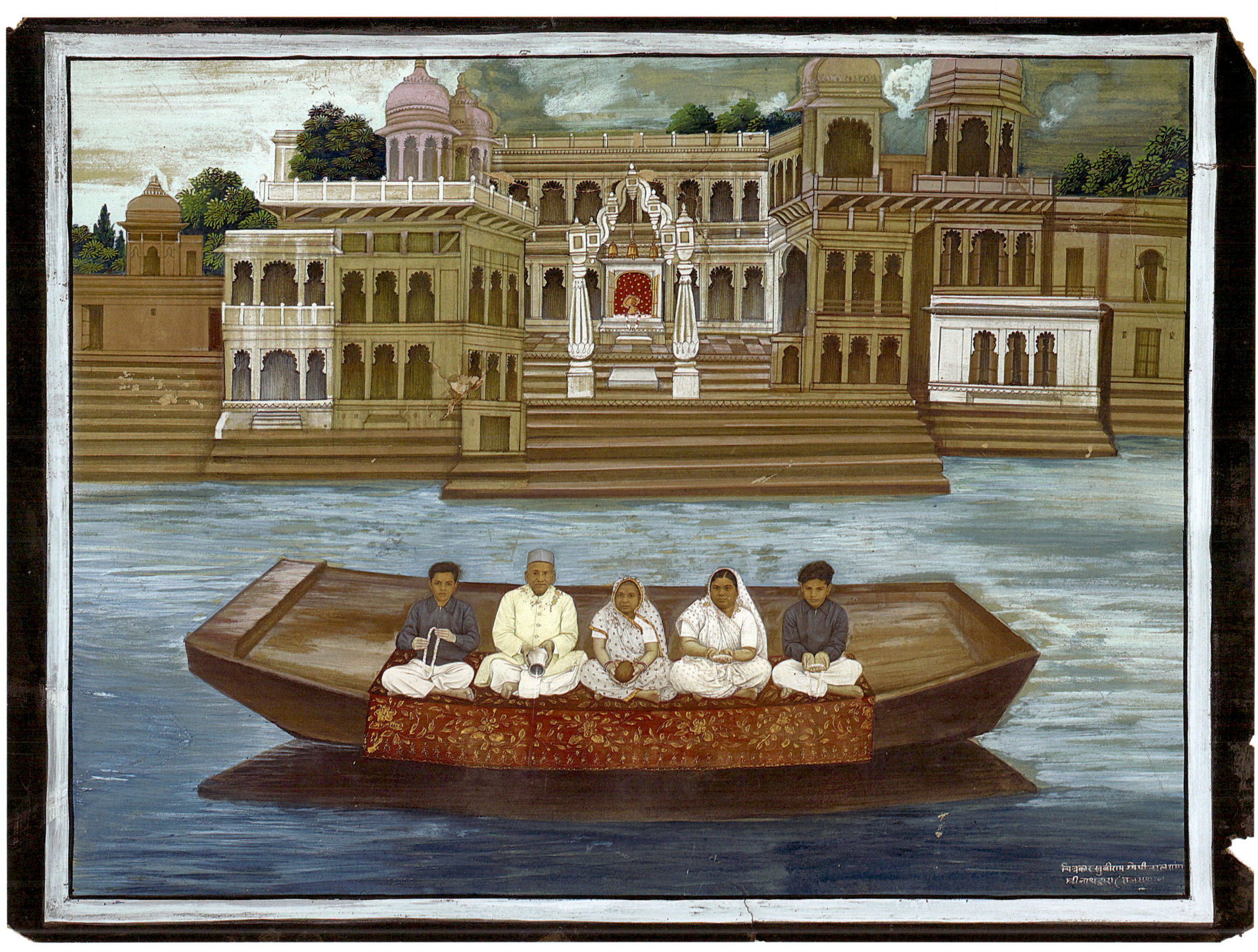

FIGURE 16.

A Pushti Marg Family on Pilgrimage at Vishram Ghat, Mathura.

By Khubiram and Gopilal;

cut-and-pasted gelatin silver prints, opaque watercolour and gold on paper; c. 1930s. 17.5 x 23.6 in. (44.4 x 59.9 cm).

Gopilal also initiated his artistic career at a very young age. After his father's death, he was sent to Udaipur to learn the art of painting under the guidance of his maternal uncle, the famous Pannalal Gaur (c. 1880–1950), who was the head of Maharana Fateh Singh's atelier. At the age of 16, he returned to Nathdwara where he opened a studio with Khubiram. Gopilal is known to have executed numerous paintings, including some of the murals of the Moti Mahal, the residence of the *tilkayat*s in Nathdwara, and to have worked for wealthy patrons outside the Pushti Marg network, such as the Nizam of Hyderabad and Sir Seth Hukumchand of Indore (1874-1959).

While both Khubiram and Gopilal were trained painters, many of the images inscribed with their names were produced by other Nathdwara artists and collaborators. Our analysis of *manorath*s suggests that Khubiram and Gopilal encouraged a traditional method of execution in which numerous individuals, each with specialized skills, would contribute to a single work. There was a painter specializing in backdrops, a photographer taking portraits of the devotees in a studio, a collaborator cutting and thinning photographs, someone in charge of arranging these on half-painted backdrops (Fig. 13a), and a professional artist responsible for finishing the portraits and the compositions. This type of cooperative work, common in the Indian painting tradition, was adopted by Khubiram and Gopilal for commercial reasons, since it allowed them to respond to the increased demand for *manorath*s, to lower their prices, and to finish their works in the fastest time possible. It was in this collaborative context that Khubiram and Gopilal put their own names on the finished works before handing them over to the commissioners.

In some of the mixed-media *manorath*s, this quasi-mechanical reproduction resulted in the repetition, or copy, of certain features. For example, Cat. nos. 21–23 have identical configurations of the inner sanctum, including the depiction of the icon of Shrinathji, the Gopashtami *pichhwai* behind it, and the portraits of two priests, Govardhanlal and his son. This correspondence suggests that a single artist was in charge of copying identical tableaux onto multiple works. Such identical tableaux in the central portion of the *manorath* can also be seen in other examples. Cat. no. 24, dated 1941, has a backdrop identical to those in two images in the collection of the Museum of Art and Photography (MAP) in Bangalore.[50] The repetition of features was not a practice adopted by Khubiram and Gopilal alone; the Govind Art Studio (Cat. no. 26) and the Bharat Art Studio (Cat. no. 18) operated in the same way. Dated examples suggest that this convention became established from the 1930s. The name of a studio inscribed on such works functions like a brand name and indicates that the atelier had gained a reputation in the Nathdwara marketplace for the production of devotional artworks.

Dated works suggest that the activities of Khubiram and Gopilal flourished in the period from the 1930s to the mid-1940s. The two partners produced and sold not only popular *manorath*s but also works in other genres such as *pichhwai*s, Krishna

50. The two works (PMA.00042 and PTG.00083) are viewable online on the museum website at map-india.org/collections/ (accessed 03 September 2018). PTG.00083 is dated 1944 and inscribed Khubiram and Gopilal. The same type of correspondence is also noticeable between Cat. no. 17 and another work by Khubiram and Gopilal in the same museum (PMA.00040).

lila paintings, and memorial portraits, on which their names likewise appear. There were also new devotional compositions that became favorite subjects at that time, such as the images of pilgrims at Vishram Ghat in Mathura. Fig. 16 is a mixed-media painting, dated to c. the 1930s and inscribed by Khubiram and Gopilal, which predates by several years two other compositions depicting the same subject. One is a c. 1960 gelatin silver print in the collection of Aditya Ruia, and the other is a Royal Ontario Museum painted photograph dated 1973.[51] The two photographs, both inscribed by the Bharat Studios of Mathura, not only attest to the popularity of this subject but also indicate the spatiotemporal span of the Pushti Marg visual network and the importance of Khubiram and Gopilal in its dissemination.

The two partners also acted as middlemen for many Nathdwara artists, putting their own names on finished works and thus nullifying the authorship of painters and photographers who sought recognition for their work.[52] These professionals were very upset by the practices of Khubiram and Gopilal. Some important evidence recording their indignation was gathered by Tryna Lyons in 1992 in a conversation with Hiralal and Kanhaiyalal, two painters who worked for the Khubiram and Gopilal workshop. She records (295) that they described this studio's activities as "*thagi* (duping or cheating)." Therefore, although inscribing a work with the names of Khubiram and Gopilal might be justifiable in the case of those *manorath*s created by a workshop of artists and photographers, the presence of this name on a refined work by a single artist raises important ethical questions and can be compared to falsification.

There are some artworks in the collection on which the names of Khubiram and Gopilal might have obscured the name of a professional artist. A curious example is Fig. 8a, a memorial portrait of Goswami Kanhaiyalal of Mathura (1868–1911), which is inscribed *Chitrakar Khubiram Sharma*, indicating the authorship of Khubiram himself. A very similar painting, in the collection of Aditya Ruia, is signed by another artist, Raghunath Sukhdev.[53] The resemblance between the two images raises important questions about Khubiram's authorship, suspicions which are legitimated by the controversial practices of his studio and further reinforced by comparing the portrayals of the devotees in Fig. 8a with another painting, Cat. no. 2, which is

51. For the gelatin silver print in the collection of Aditya Ruia, see Ruia, fig. 14. For the painted photograph in the ROM collection, see Dewan, *Embellished Reality*, cat. no. 58.

52. For Khubiram and Gopilal as middlemen, see Ambalal, *Krishna as Shrinathji* 90–91; and Lyons 229, 295.

53. See Ruia, fig. 4.

inscribed, once again, with the name of Raghunath Sukhdev. The unquestionable stylistic similarities of the human figures in these works justify the attribution of Fig. 8a to Raghunath rather than Khubiram. The characteristics of another image, Cat. no. 31, lead us to think it was executed by a professional artist whose name was obscured by Khubiram and Gopilal. This case is considered below.

In the photographic studio

The collection holds a small number of painted photographs which also belong to the *manorath* genre. The earliest and most elaborate of them is Cat. no. 31, a gelatin silver print painted in oil colours which can be dated to the 1930s. The background of the original print, which was probably plain, has been transformed into a romanticized interior of the Nathdwara temple, including pillars, draped curtains, and cusped arches. The two devotees stand next to a fountain. Behind them is a polylobed arch framing the icon of Shrinathji. This heavily painted photograph indicates that the artist intended to create a new work rather than simply to enhance the original black-and-white photograph. The indexicality of the photograph is subverted to produce an entirely different and idiosyncratic work which retains very little trace of its prototype. Its composition and ornamentation are complex, and devoid of the repetitiveness of the commercial *manoraths* seen above, suggesting it was painted by a professional artist. The work is inscribed *Chitrakar Khubiram Gopilal Sharma.* Considering the questionable practices of this atelier, Cat. no. 31 may well represent another example in which the studio name conceals the identity of the actual author.

Another painted photograph belonging to the *manorath* genre is Cat. no. 34. This can be compared with the previous one in order to help us understand the different modalities in which painted photographs were finished, either by covering their entire surfaces with colours to modify the prototypes (Cat. no. 31), or else by enhancing the original sources. The latter process was used in Cat. no. 34, which is lightly tinted to embellish the black-and-white print, which nevertheless remains clearly visible. The devotees are painted over to beautify their figures and clothes. The studio backdrop against which they pose is plain and the sanctum of the Nathdwara temple is indicated by a prop representing Shrinathji. The icon is heavily painted in such a way as to recall older *manoraths*.

Between the 1950s and the 1970s, black-and-white gelatin silver prints became a favorite medium for *manorath* images. The collection owns three of them. Cat. no. 32 is posed in an exterior setting and accommodates a large group of Pushti Marg followers. An interesting feature of this *manorath* is that the photographer, Narendra Kumar Paliwal, has modified the glass negative with paint in order to add clouds and leafy branches, which appear in white in the printed version. This expedient serves to fill the blank space behind the group and renders the composition livelier. In Cat. nos. 33 and 35, the pilgrims pose in a studio next to a prop depicting the icon of Shrinathji. Cat. no. 33 even introduces the Nathdwara temple roof at the top of the composition, an iconographic detail reminiscent of traditional miniature paintings. These later examples suggest that black-and-white photographic *manorath*s gained momentum and eclipsed the colourful mixed-media ones by around the late 1950s. At that time, photographers replicated in the studio the iconographic conventions of earlier painted models, allowing devotees to adopt appropriate devotional poses next to a prop representing Shrinathji. Cat. no. 35 is dated 1976, indicating the long historic span in which the *manorath* genre flourished.[54]

The history of the *manorath* genre starts with miniature painting at the beginning of the century, evolves with the incorporation of new media and technologies from the 1920s, and sees the full embrace of the black-and-white and tinted photography from the late 1950s onward. In the course of this development, the genre always remained faithful to the prototypical painted *manorath*s of the early twentieth century and retained the devotional meaning expected by its Pushti Marg audiences.

54. For a photographic *manorath* dated c. 1994, see Pinney, *Photos of the Gods*, fig. 72.

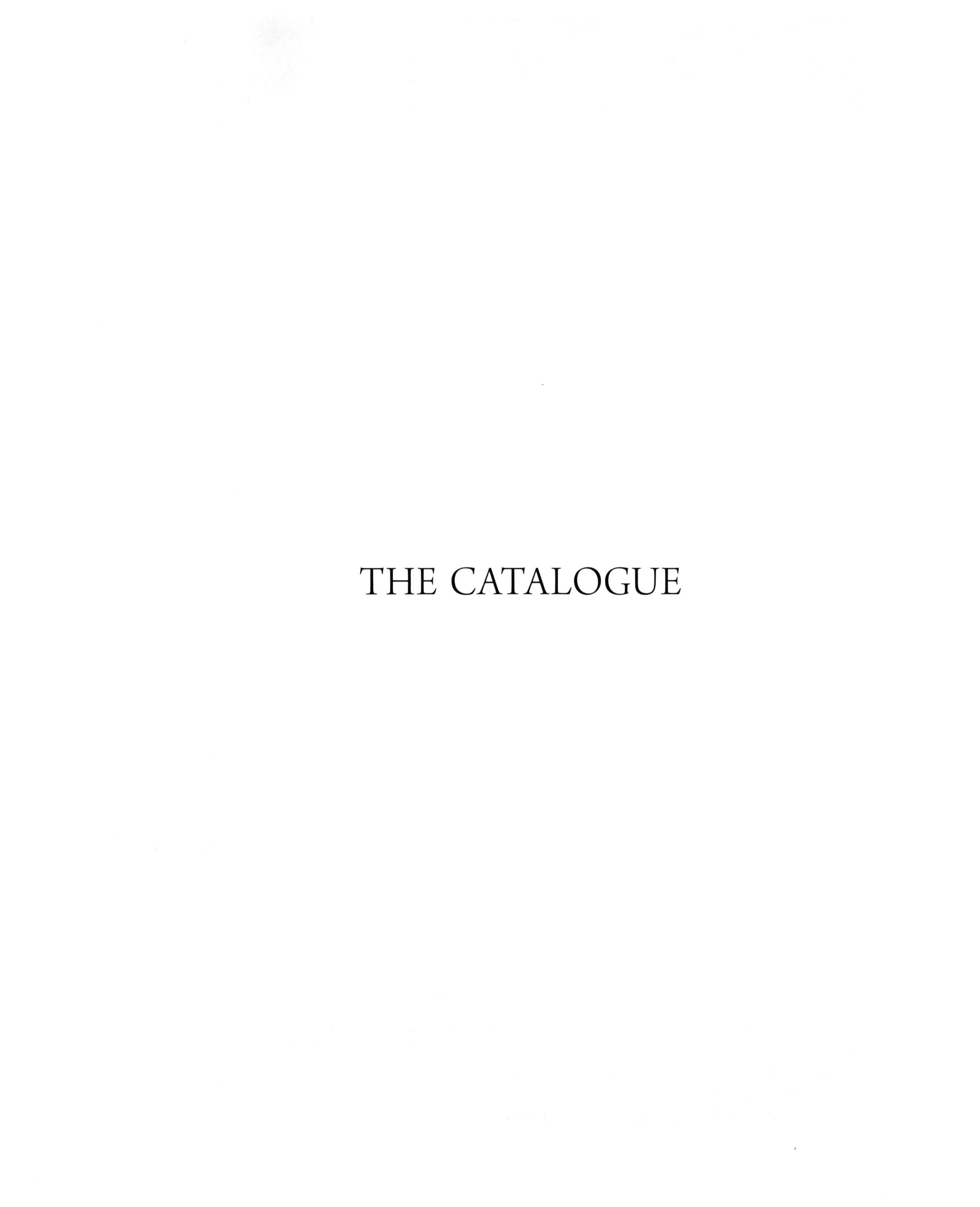

THE CATALOGUE

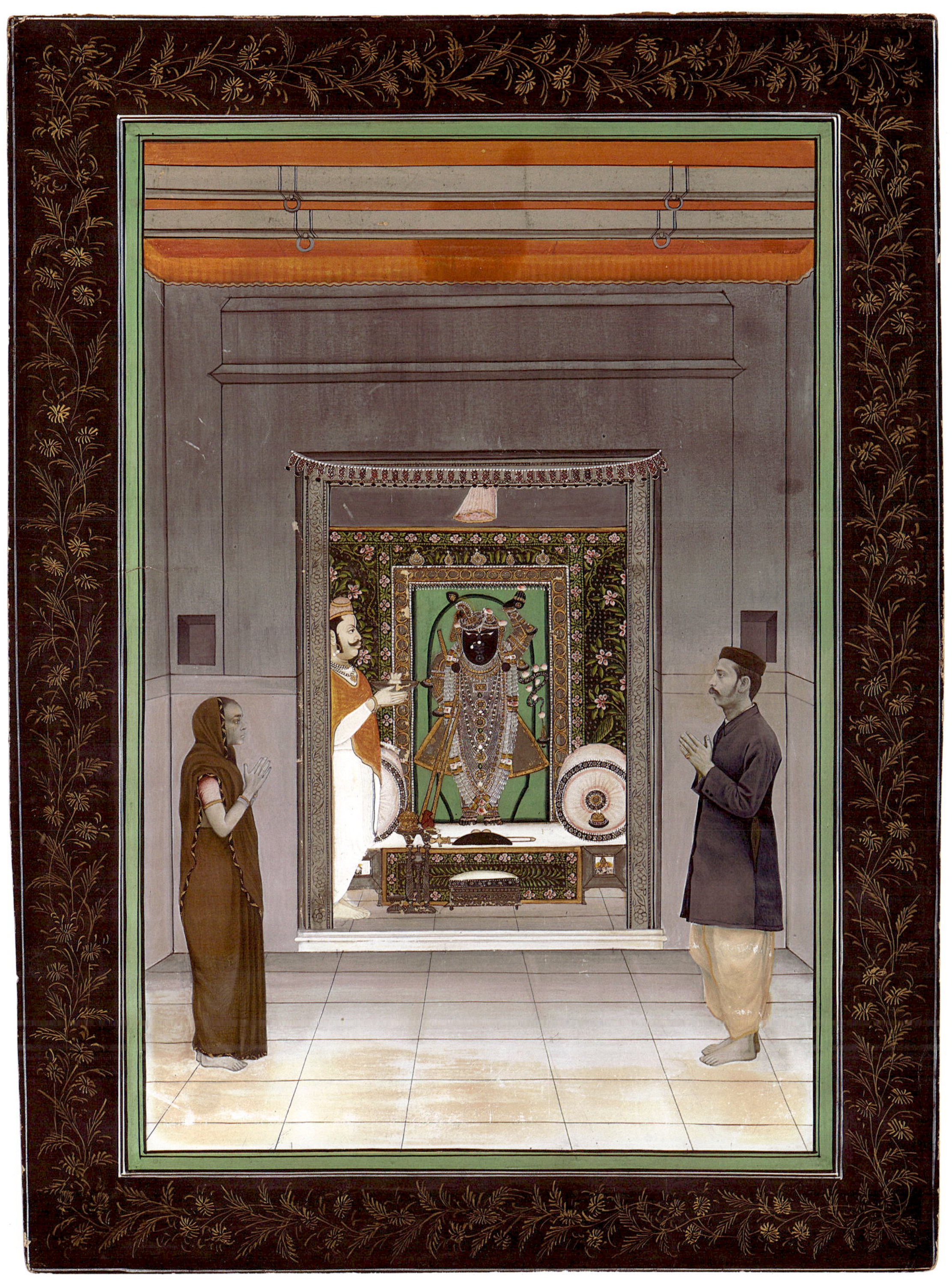

1. *Manorath* Performed by Govardhanlal on the Occasion of Dussehra.
Ghasiram Hardev Sharma.

Opaque watercolour, gold and silver on paper; c. 1900–1910.
17.75 x 12.75 in. (45.1 x 32.4 cm).

Inscribed in English on the verso: *Painter Ghasiram Nathdwara*

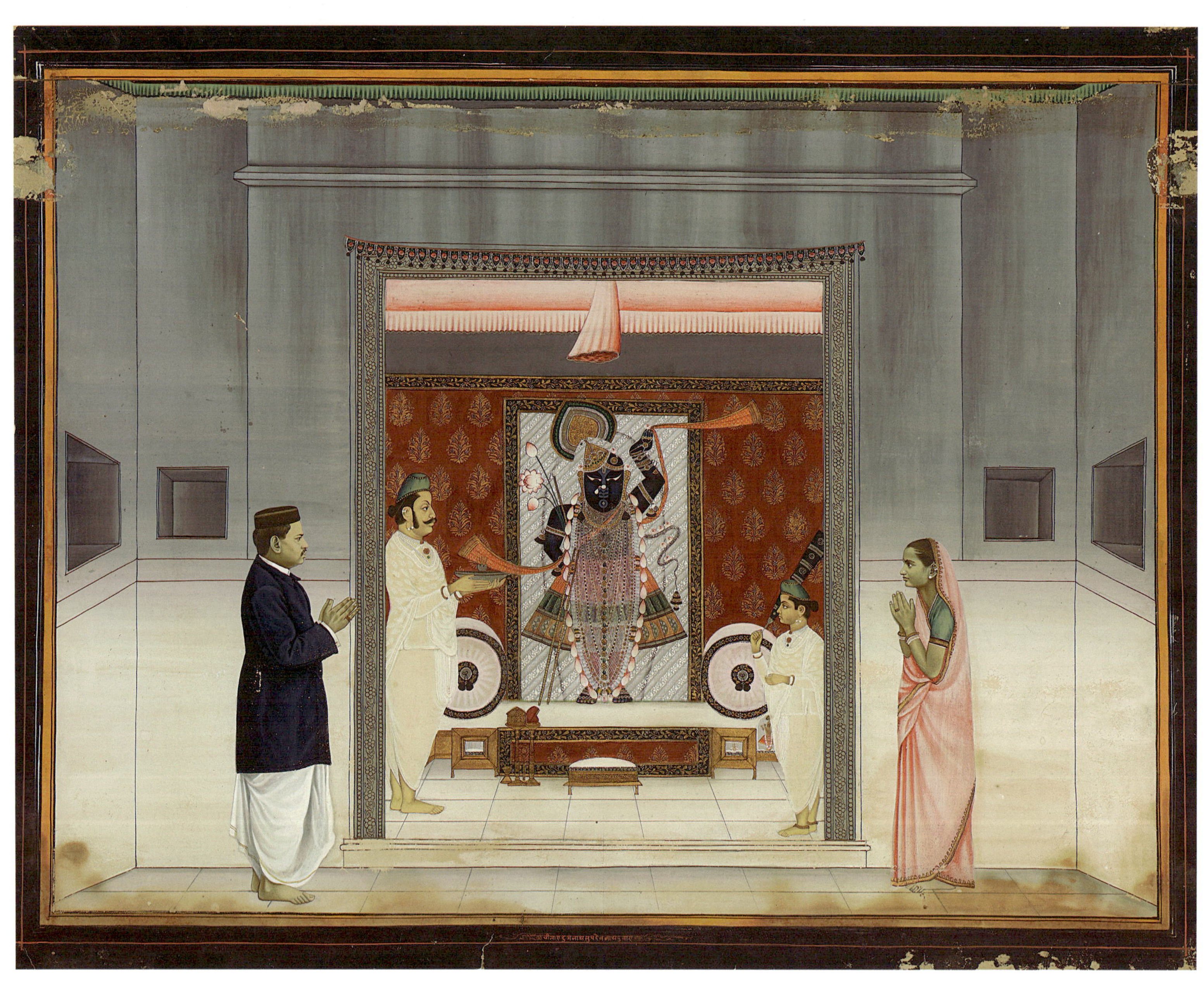

2. *Manorath* Performed by Govardhanlal and a Young Priest.
Raghunath Sukhdev.

Opaque watercolour, gold and silver on paper; c. 1910.
19.7 x 24.2 in. (50 x 61.5 cm).

Inscribed in Hindi on the recto: *cītārā rugnāth sukhdev nāthduvār*

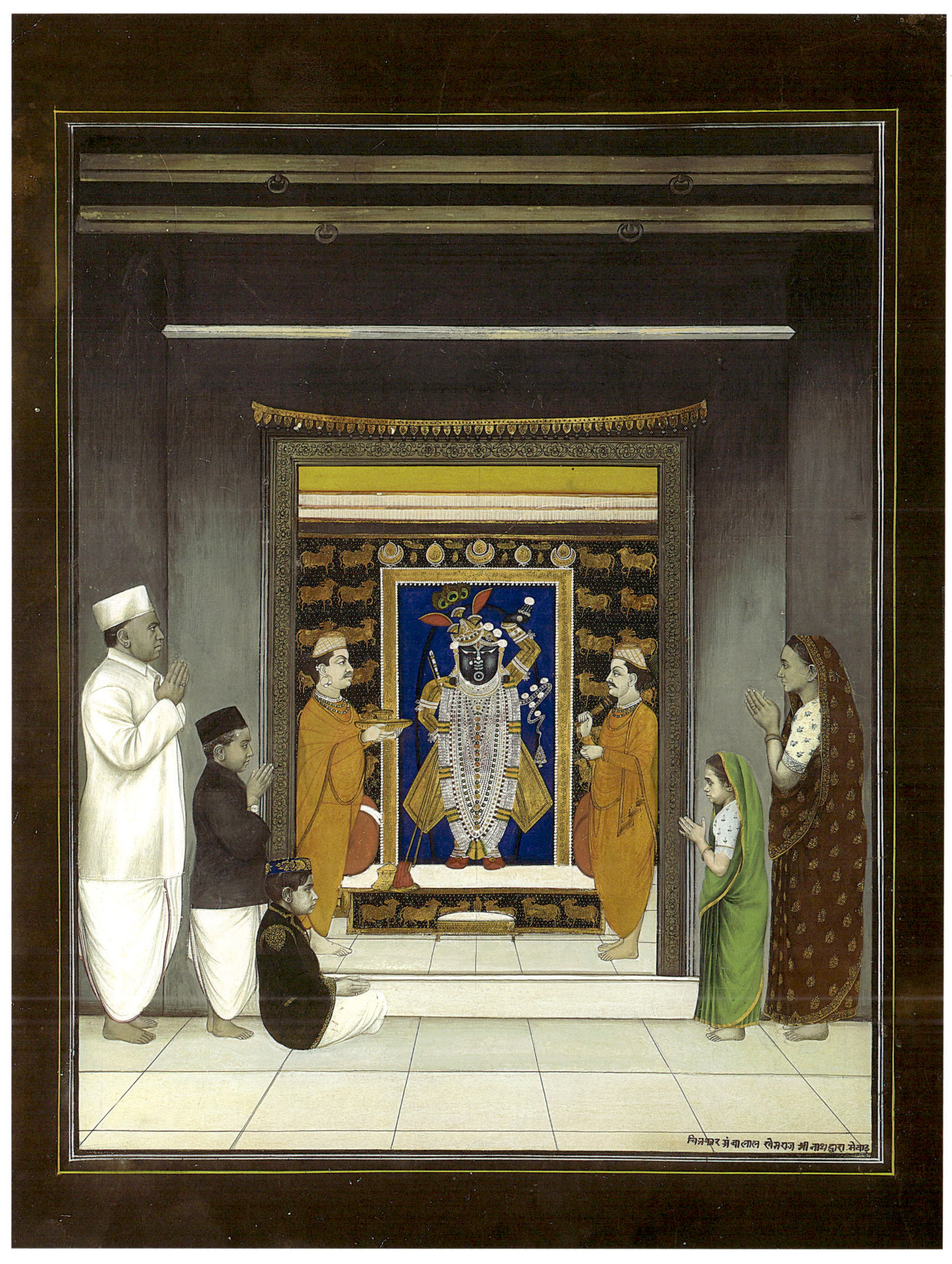

3. *Manorath* Performed by Govardhanlal and Damodarlal on the Occasion of Gopashtami.
Ambalal Khemraj.

Opaque watercolour and gold on paper; c. 1920.
23.5 x 17.8 in. (60 x 45.1 cm).

Inscribed in Hindi on the recto: *citrkār aṃbālāl khemrāj śrī nāthdvārā mevāḍ*

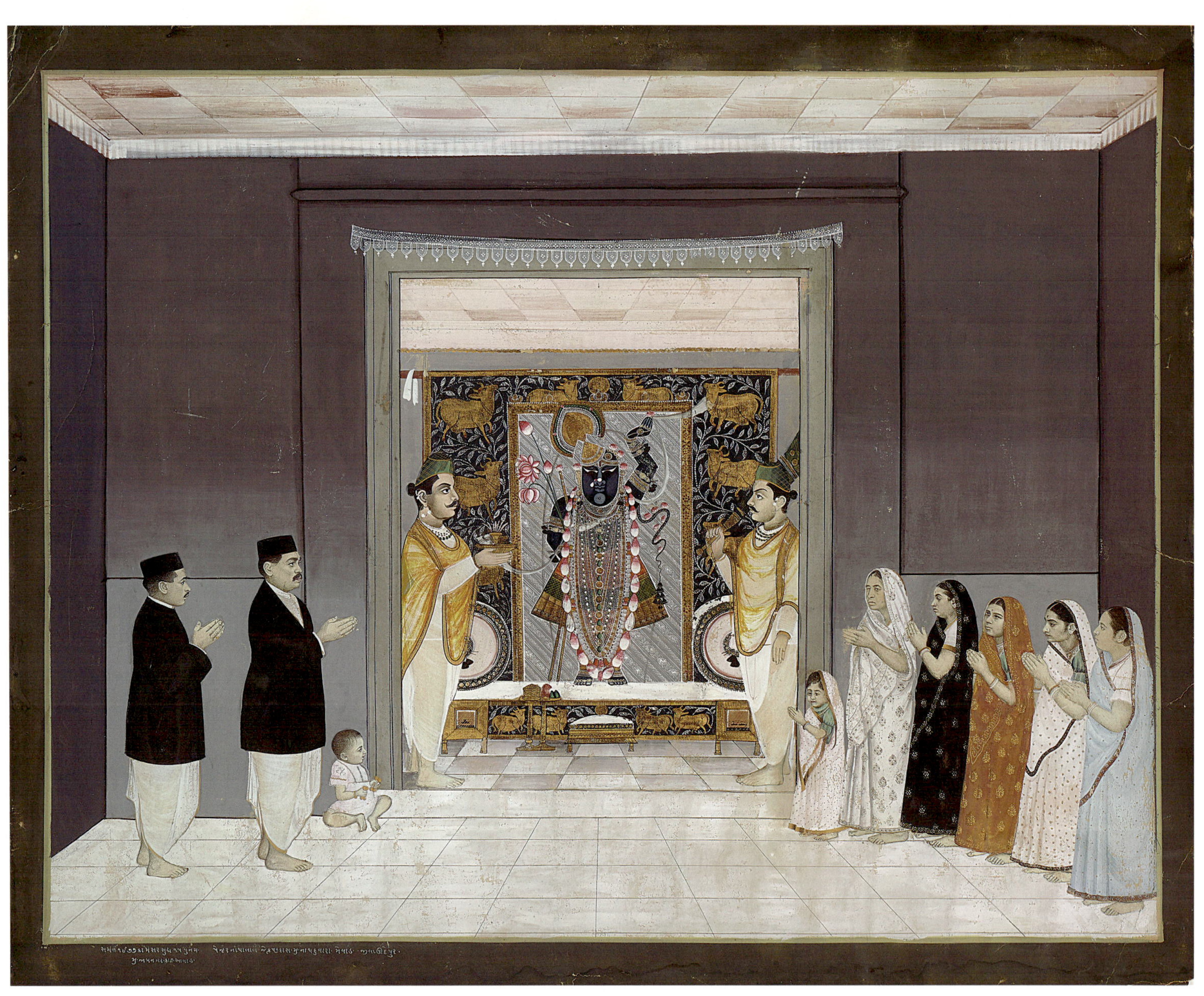

4. *Manorath* with a Family from Jamnagar, Gujarat, on the Occasion of Gopashtami.
Nathalal Jaikrishnadas.

Opaque watercolour and gold on paper; dated 1920.
20 x 24 in. (50.8 x 61 cm).

Inscribed in Gujarati on the recto: *samat 1977 kāmsar sudh 15 punam / peṇṭar nāthālāl jekṛṣṇdās mu. nāthduvārā mevāḍ jīlā ūdepur // mu. jamnagar kāṭhīāvāḍ*

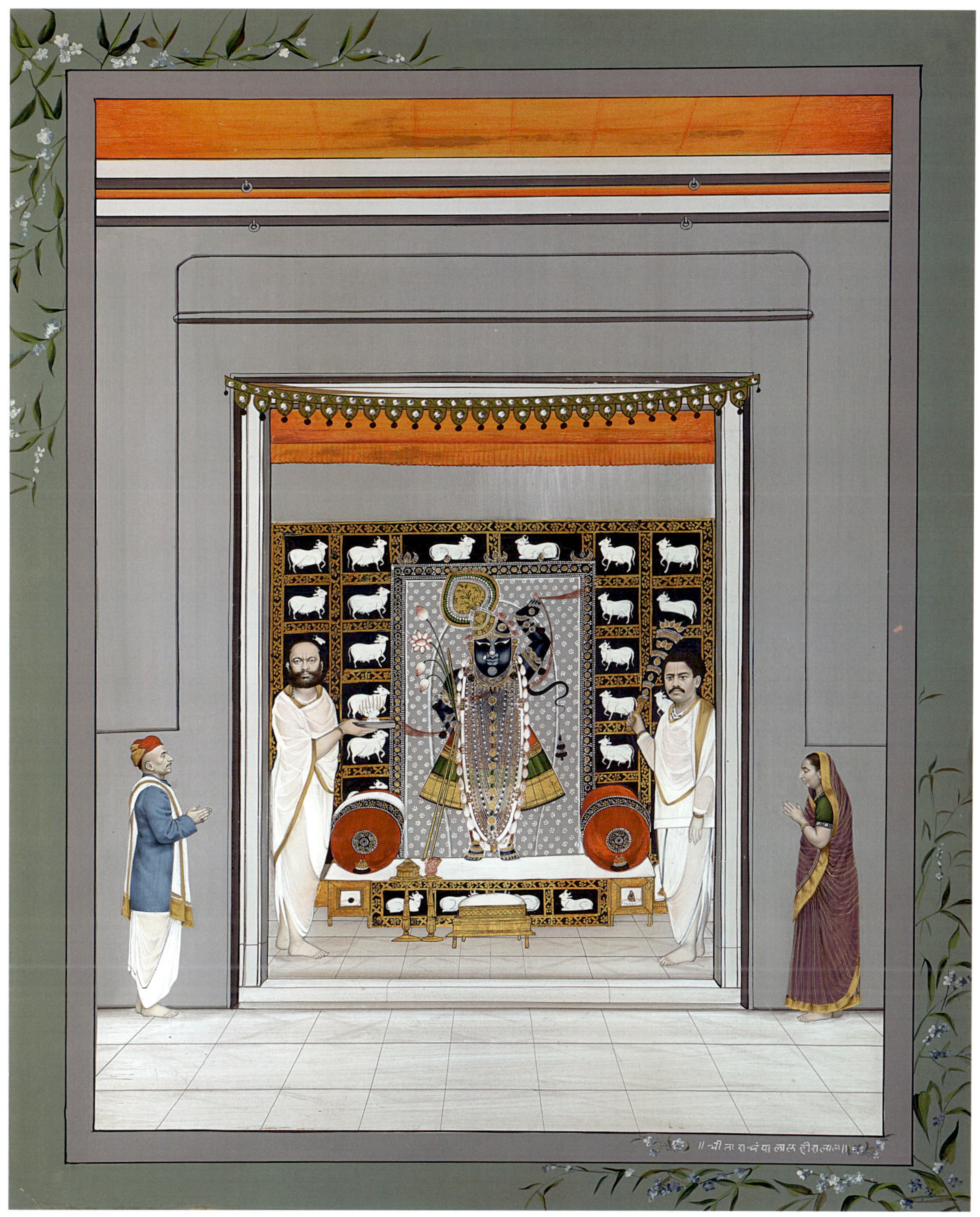

5. *Manorath* Performed by Maganlal of Surat (left) and his Son Vrajratanlal.
Champalal Hiralal Gaur.

Opaque watercolour and gold on paper; c. mid-1920s.
24.8 x 20 in. (63 x 50.5 cm).

Inscribed in Hindi on the recto: *citārā caṁpālāl hīrālāl*

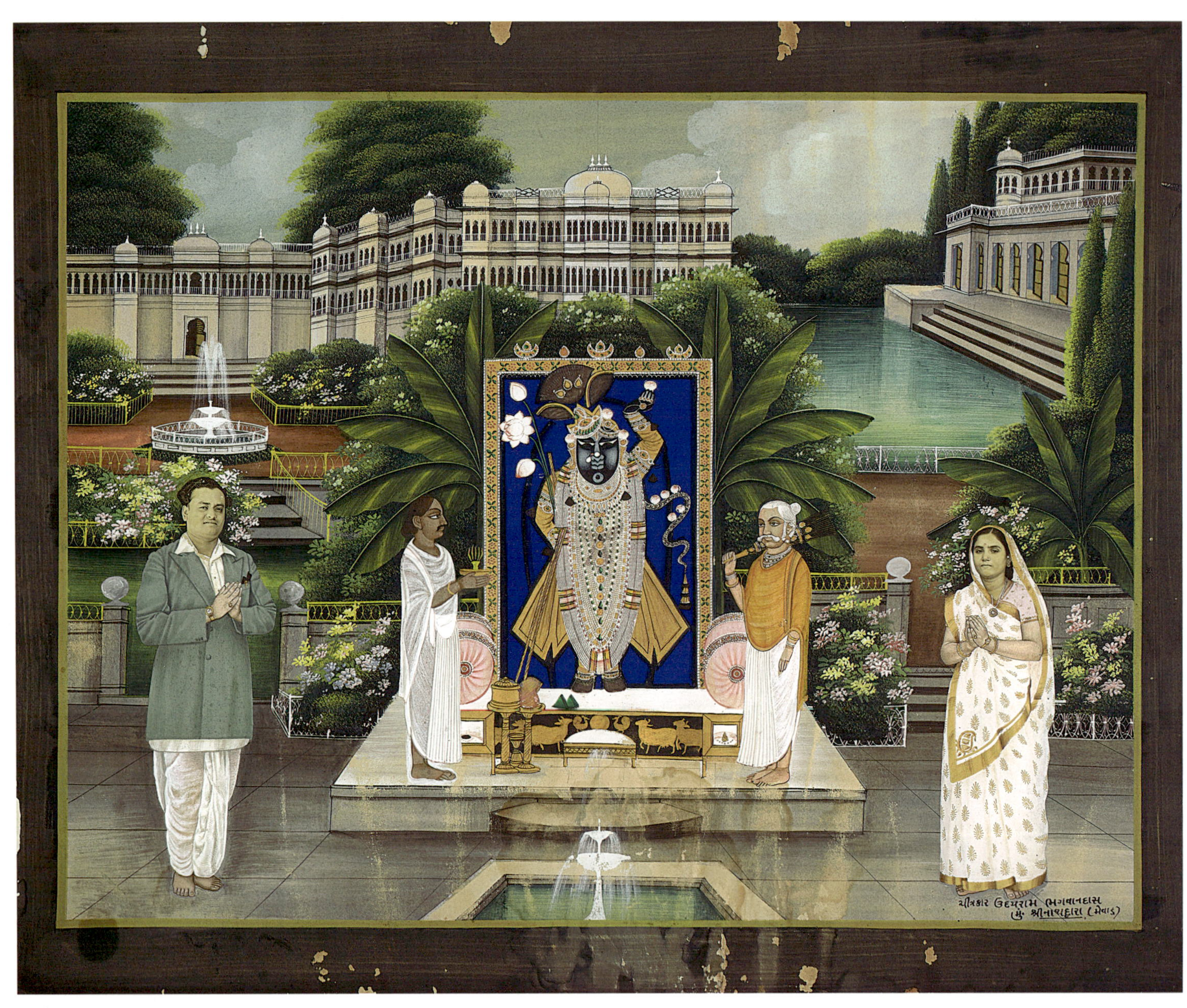

6. *Manorath* of Shrinathji with a Gujarati Couple in a Garden Setting.
Udairam Bhagvandas.

Cut-and-pasted gelatin silver prints, opaque watercolour and gold on paper; c. 1920.
20 x 24 in. (50.8 x 61 cm).

Inscribed in Gujarati on the recto: *cītrkār udayrām bhagvāndās // mu. śrīnāthdvārā (mevāḍ)*

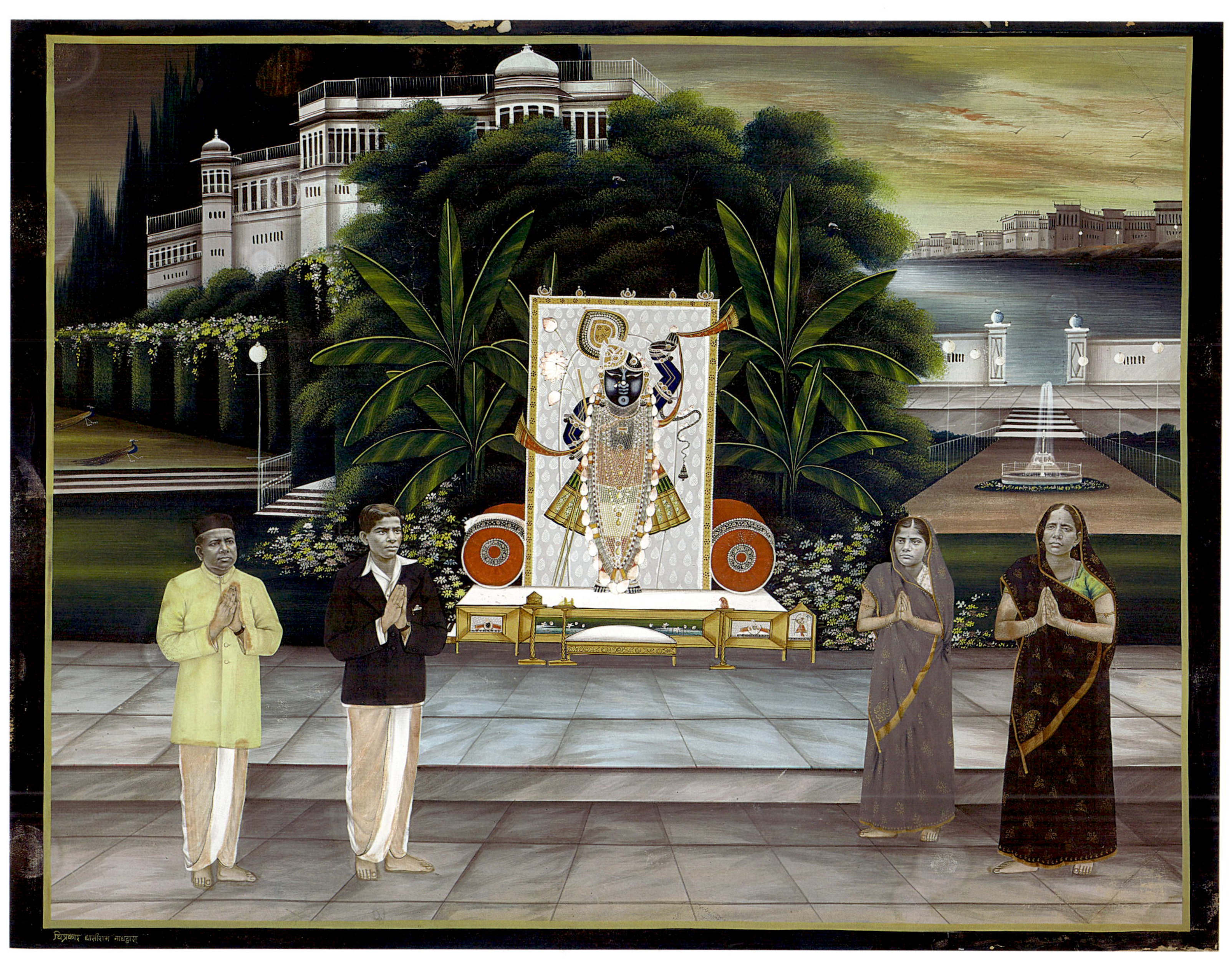

7. *Manorath* of Shrinathji with Gujarati Devotees in a Garden Setting.
Ghasiram Hardev Sharma.

Cut-and-pasted gelatin silver prints, opaque watercolour and gold on paper; c. 1925–1930.
18 x 23.8 in. (45.7 x 60.5 cm).

Inscribed in Hindi on the recto: *citrkār ghāsīrām nāthdvārā*

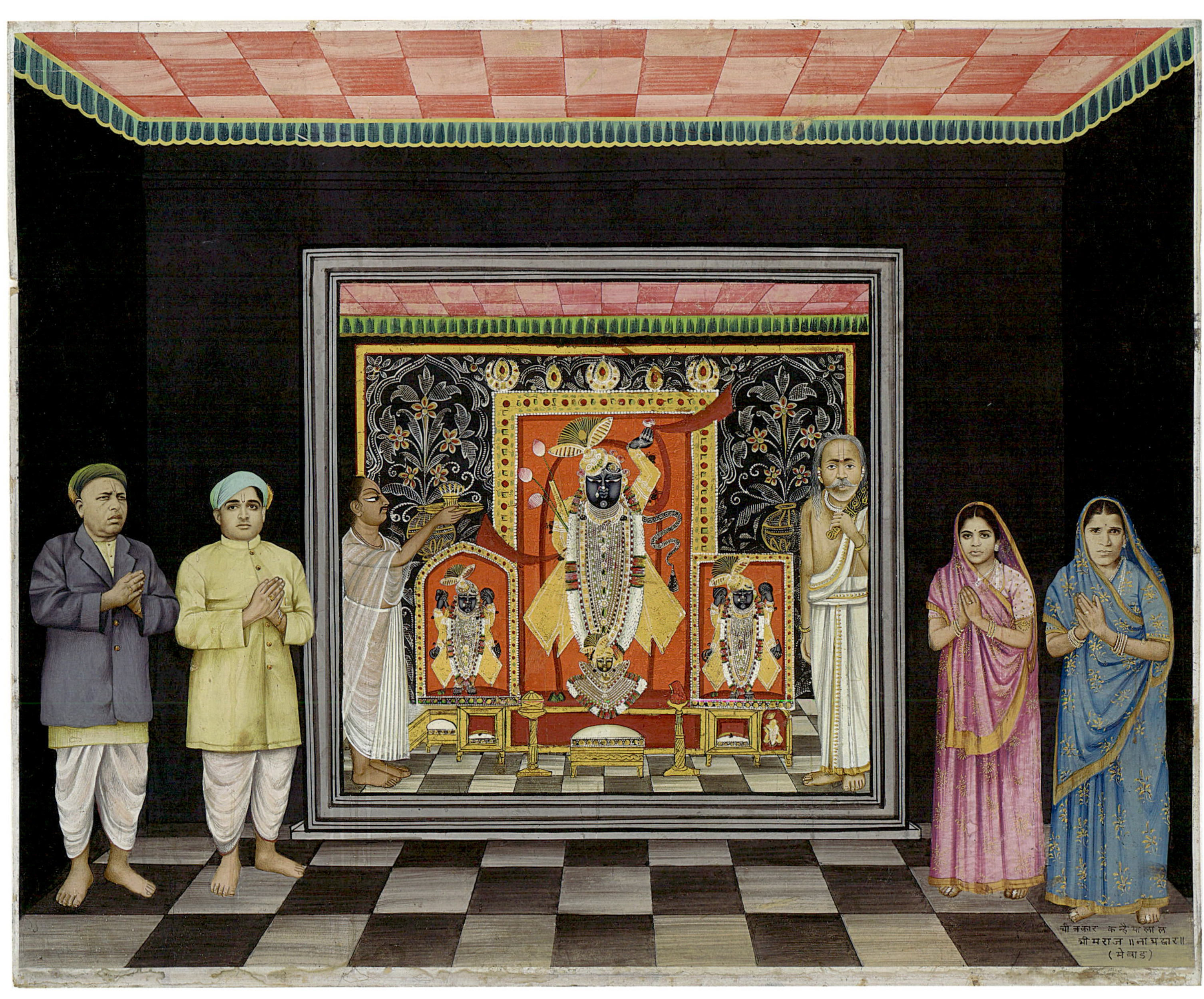

8. *Manorath* Performed by Goswami Ranchhorlal of Kota.

Kanhaiyalal Bhimraj.

Cut-and-pasted gelatin silver prints, opaque watercolour and gold on paper; c. mid-1920s.
19.5 x 23.8 in. (49.5 x 60.5 cm).

Inscribed in Hindi on the recto: *cītrkār kanhaiyālāl // bhīmrāj. nāthdvār. // (mevāḍ)*

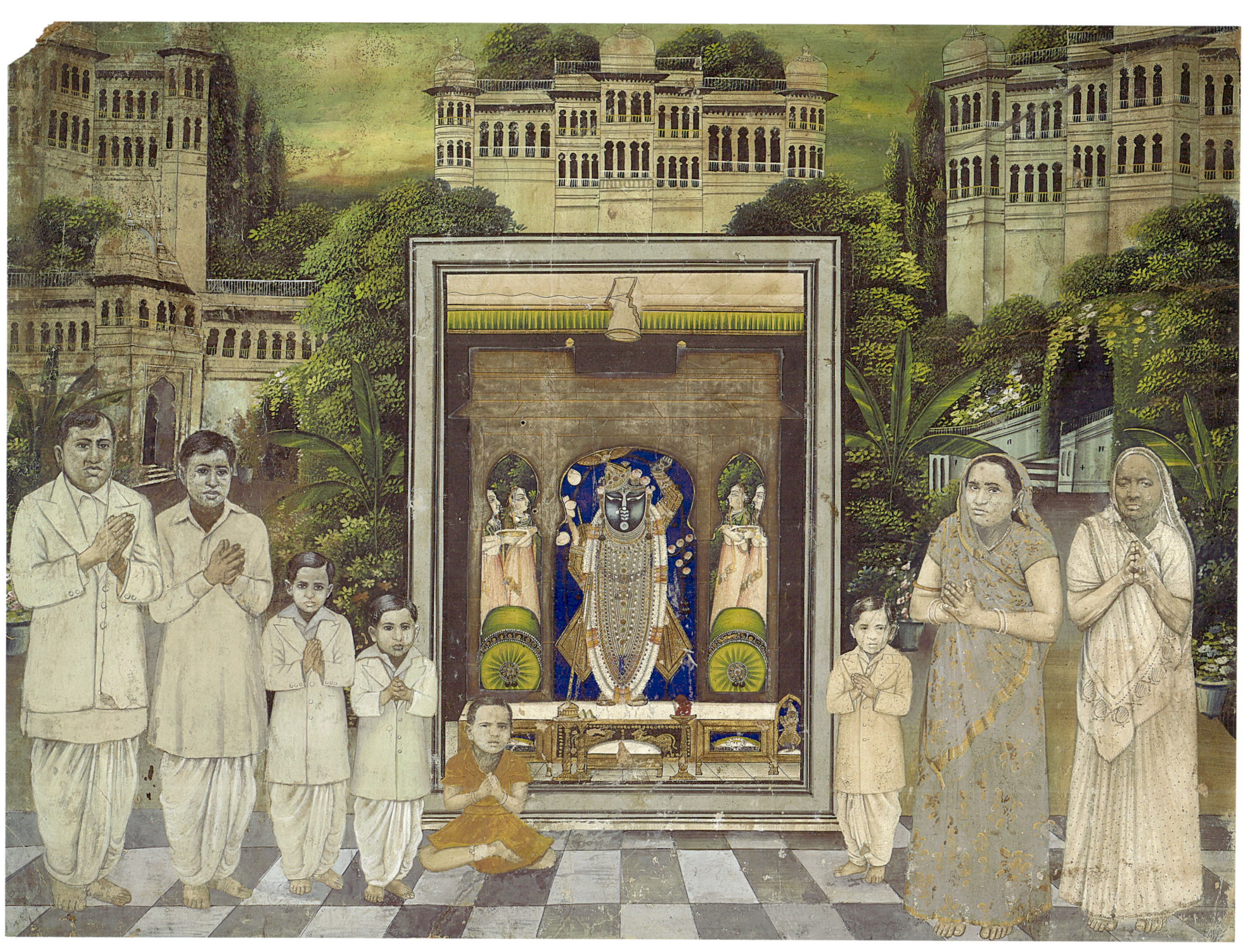

9. *Manorath* with a Family of Devotees in a Palatial Setting.
Unknown artist or studio.
Cut-and-pasted gelatin silver prints, opaque watercolour and gold on paper; c. 1930s.
16 x 21.5 in. (40.6 x 54.6 cm).

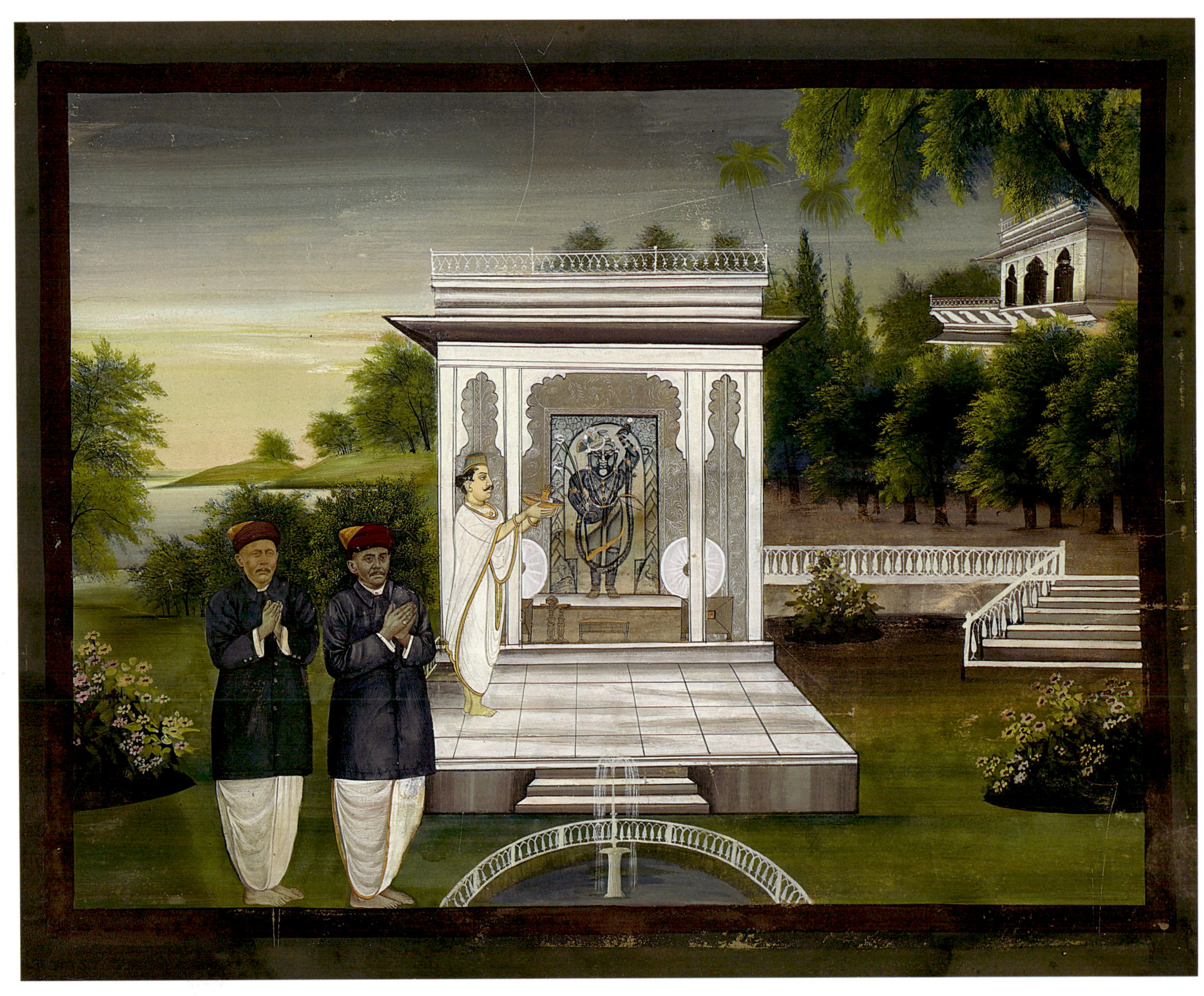

10. *Manorath* with Two Gujarati Devotees Next to a White Marble Pavilion.
Unknown artist or studio.

Cut-and-pasted gelatin silver prints, opaque watercolour and gold on paper; c. 1930s.
17.9 x 22 in. (45.5 x 55.9 cm).

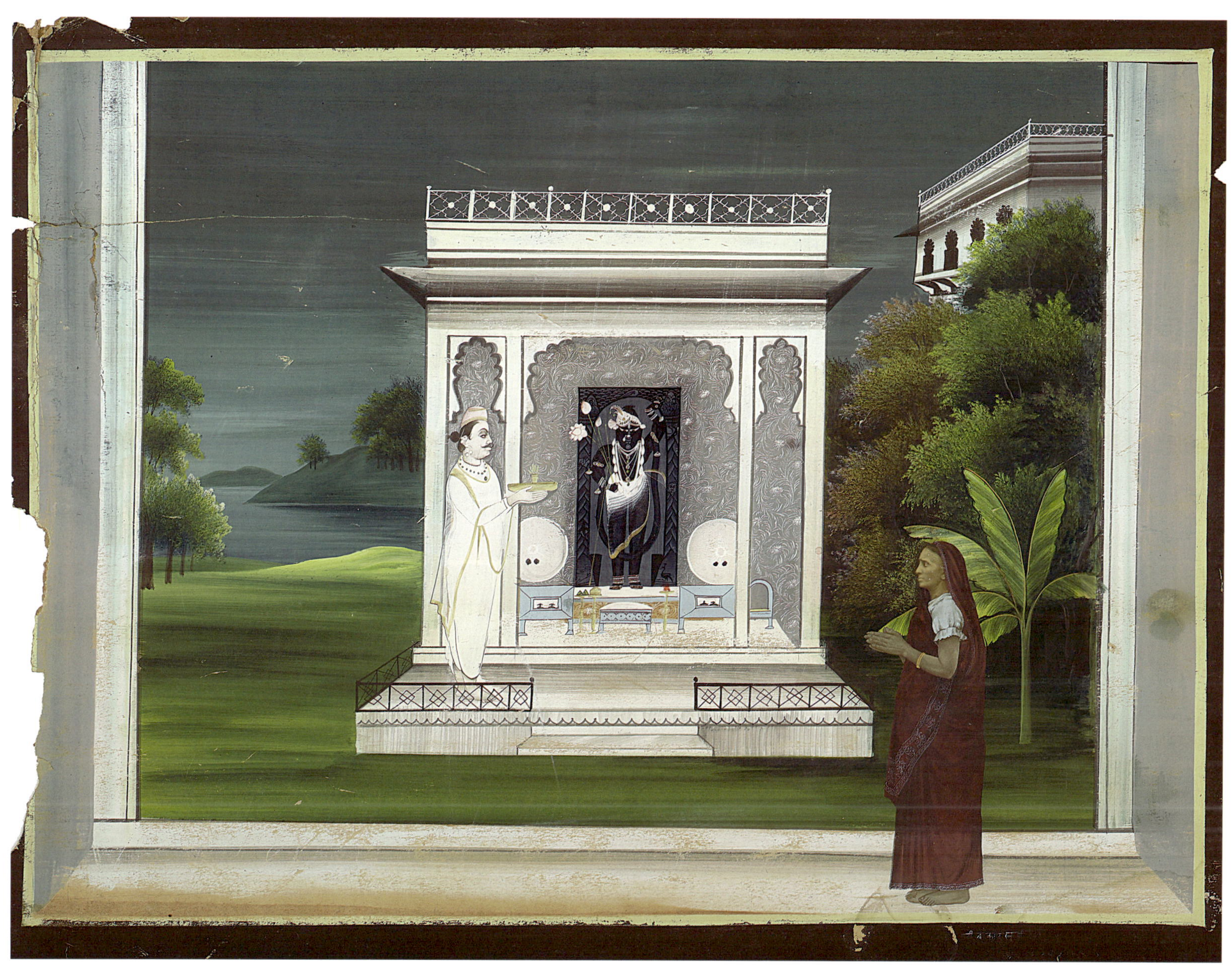

11. *Manorath* with a Woman Next to a White Marble Pavilion.
Attributed to Khubiram and Gopilal.

Cut-and-pasted gelatin silver prints, opaque watercolour and gold on paper; c. 1930s.
18.7 x 24 in. (47.5 x 61 cm).

Obliterated inscription in Hindi on the recto: *cītrkār khubī… [illegible]*

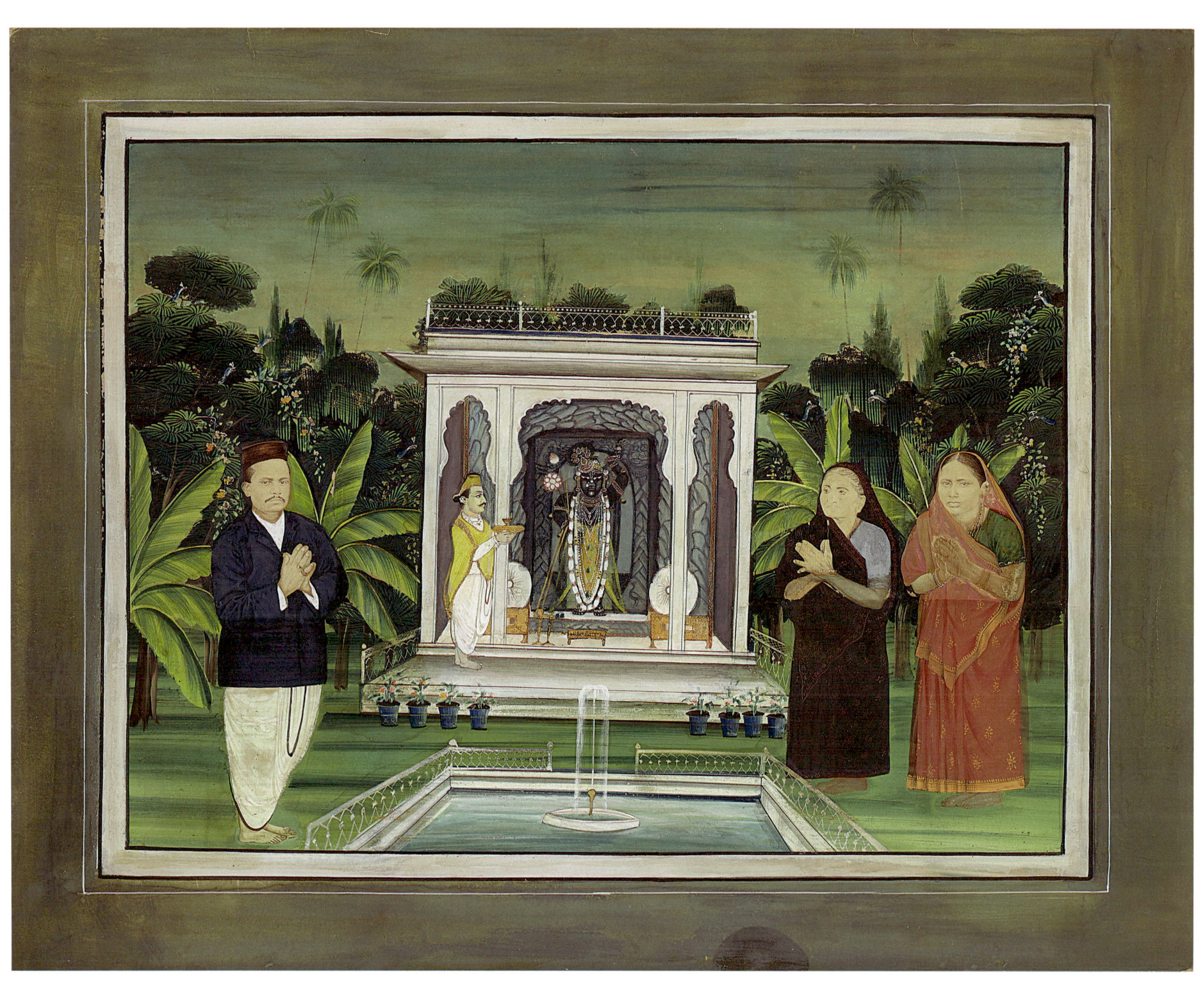

12. *Manorath* with Devotees Next to a White Marble Pavilion.
Unknown artist or studio.

Cut-and-pasted gelatin silver prints, opaque watercolour and gold on paper; c. 1930s.
20 x 25 in (50.8 x 63.5 cm).

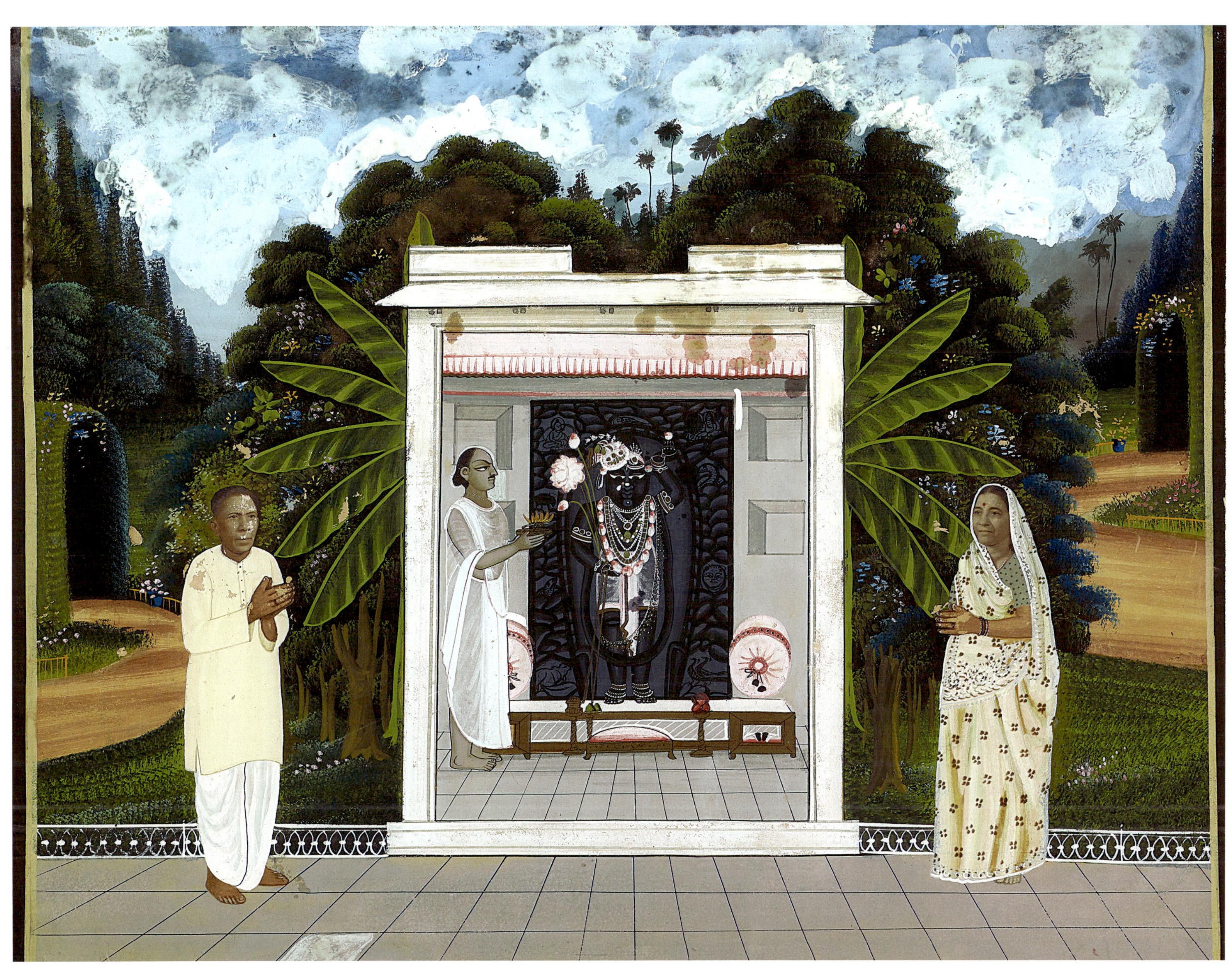

13. *Manorath* with a Couple Next to a White Marble Pavilion.
Unknown artist or studio.
Cut-and-pasted gelatin silver prints, opaque watercolour and gold on paper; c. 1930s.
18 x 23 in. (45.7 x 58.4 cm).

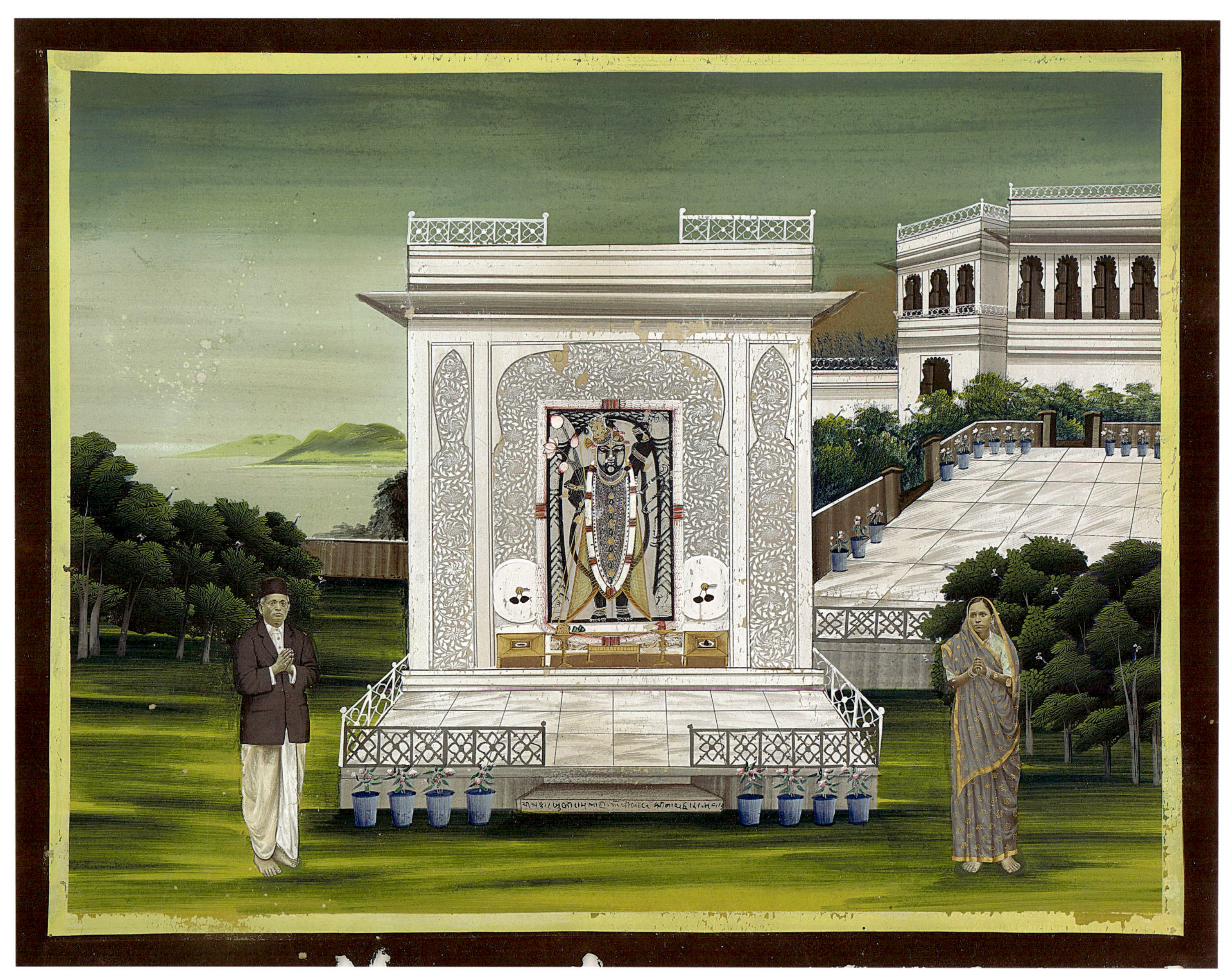

14. *Manorath* with a Couple Next to a White Marble Pavilion.
Khubiram and Gopilal.

Cut-and-pasted gelatin silver prints, opaque watercolour and gold on paper; c. 1930s.
18.9 x 23.8 in. (48 x 60.5 cm).

Inscribed in Gujarati on the recto: *cītrkār khubīrām bhāī gopīlāl śrīnāthdvārā mevāḍ*

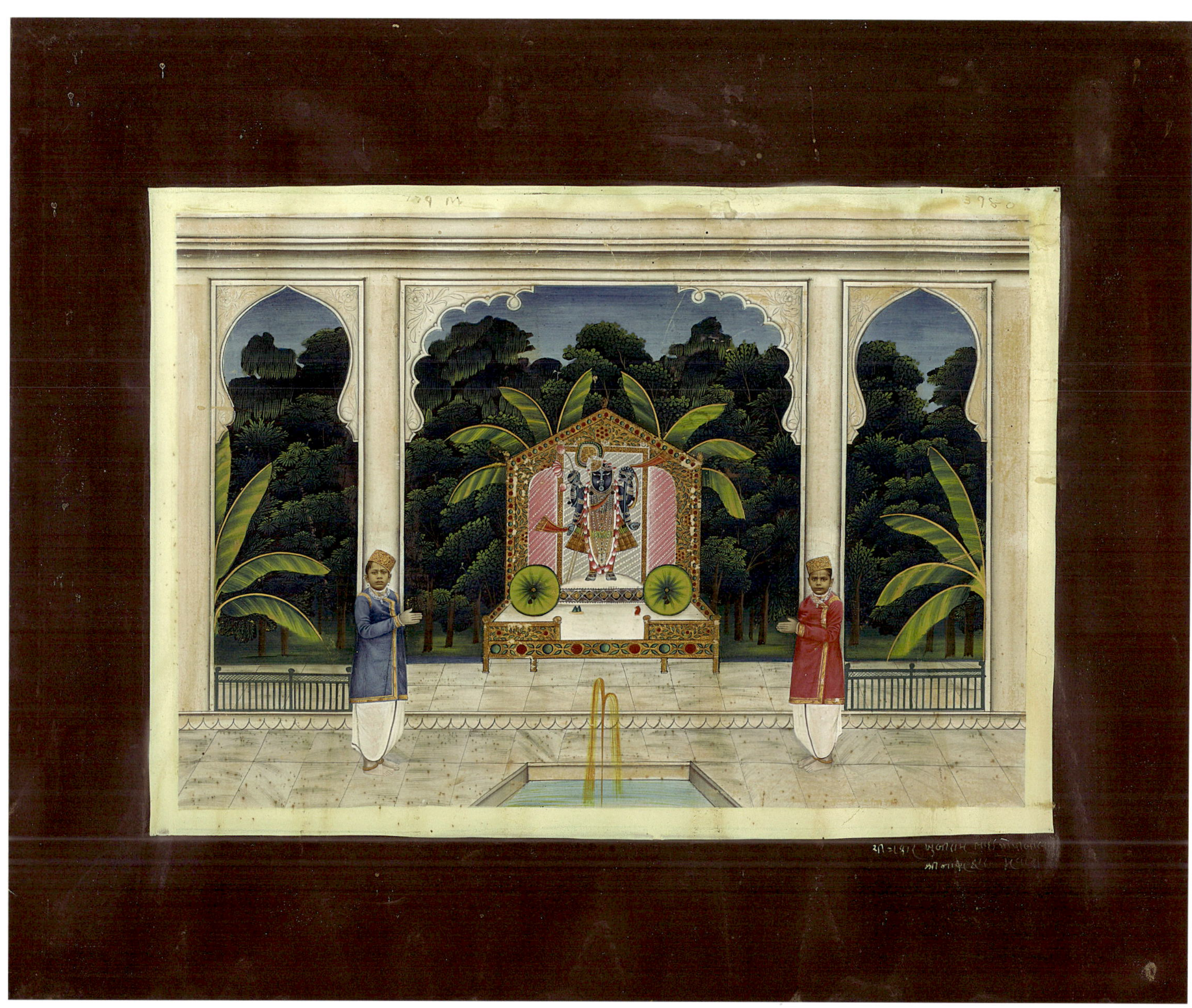

15. *Manorath* of Dwarkadishji of Kankroli with Young Boys in a Garden Pavilion.
Khubiram and Gopilal.

Cut-and-pasted gelatin silver prints, opaque watercolour and gold on paper; c. 1930s.
20.1 x 24 in (51.1 x 61 cm).

Inscribed in Gujarati on the recto: *cītrkār khubīrām bhāī gopīlāl // śrīnāthdvārā mevāḍ*.
Inscribed in Gujarati on the verso: *cītrkār // khubīrām go // pīlāl śrīnāth // dvārā mevāḍ*

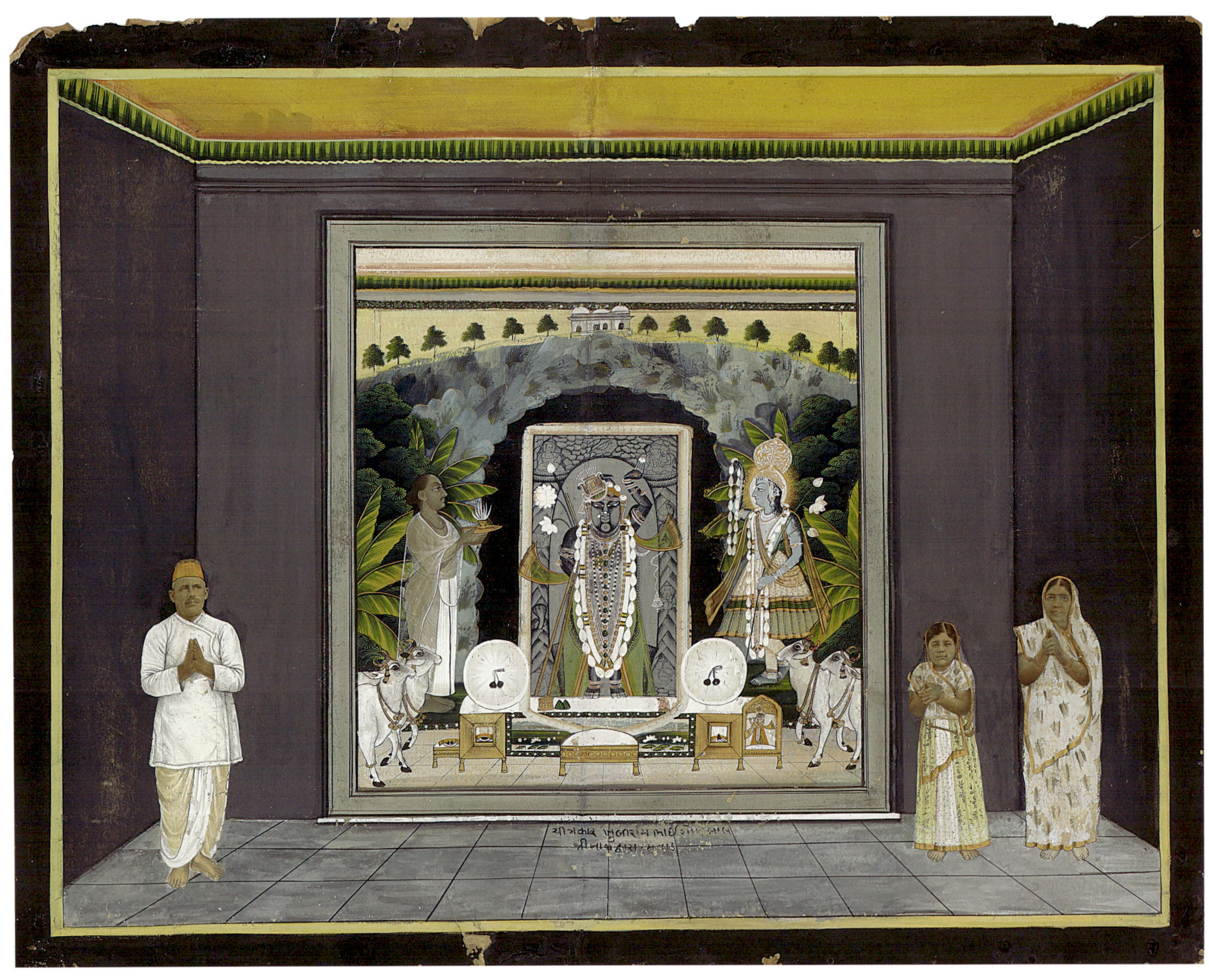

16. *Manorath* of Shrinathji with a *Pichhwai* Representing Mount Govardhan.
Khubiram and Gopilal.

Cut-and-pasted gelatin silver prints, opaque watercolour and gold on paper; c. 1930s.
20 x 24.8 in. (50.5 x 63 cm).

Inscribed in Gujarati on the recto: *citrkār khubīrām bhāī gopīlāl // śrīnāthdvārā mevāḍ*

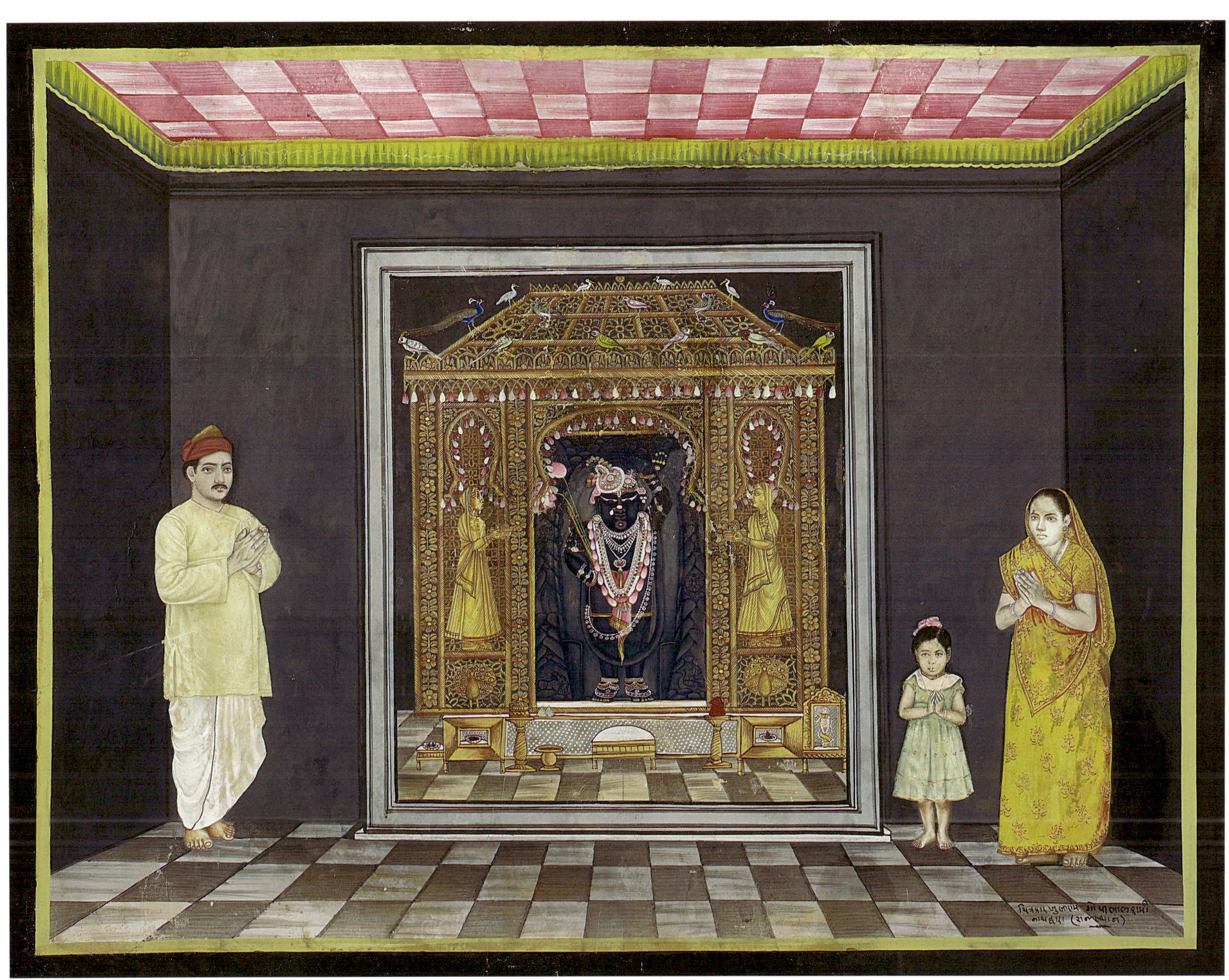

17. *Manorath* of Shrinathji in a Summer Pavilion.
Khubiram and Gopilal.
Cut-and-pasted gelatin silver prints, opaque watercolour and gold on paper; c. 1930s.
19 x 23.75 in. (48.3 x 60.3 cm).
Inscribed in Gujarati on the recto: *citrkār khubīrām gopīlāl śarmā // nāthdvārā (rājasthān)*

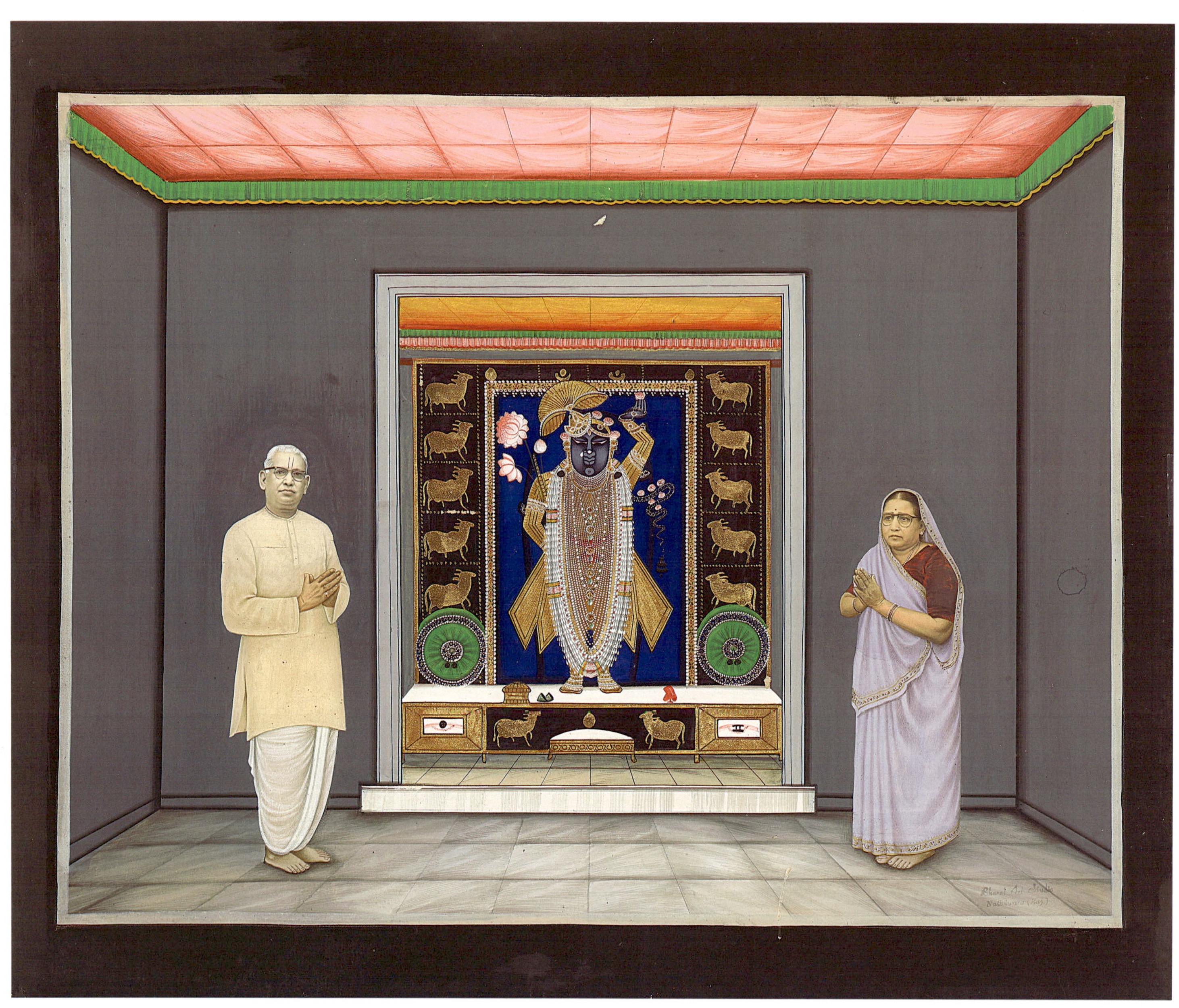

18. *Manorath* on the Occasion of Gopashtami.
Bharat Art Studio, Nathdwara.

Cut-and-pasted gelatin silver prints, opaque watercolour and gold on paper; c. 1930s.
19.7 x 23 in. (50 x 58.4 cm).

Rubber-stamped on the recto: *Bharat Art Studio // Nathdwara (Raj.)*

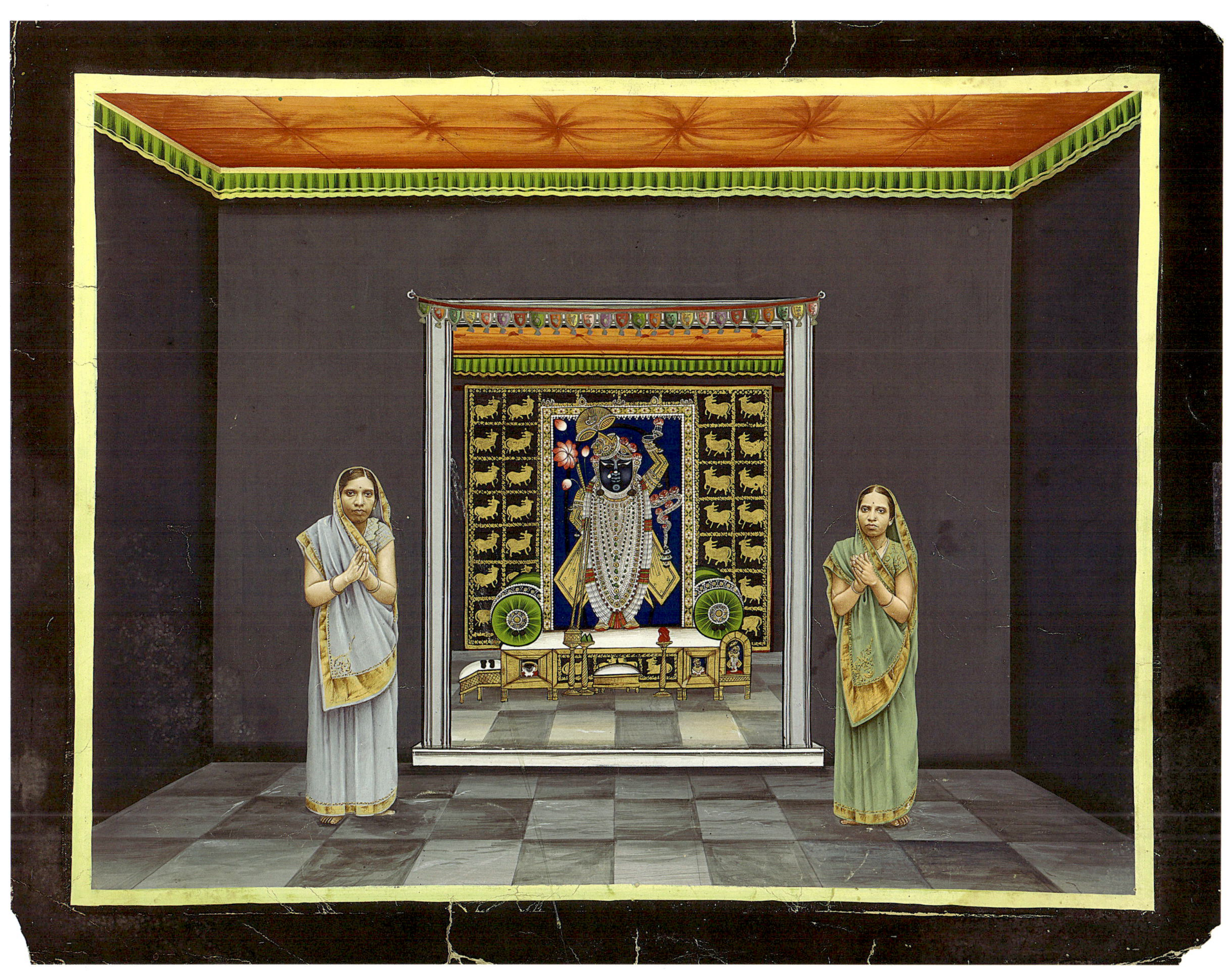

19. *Manorath* with Two Sisters on the Occasion of Gopashtami.
Attributed to Bhuralal Motilalnath Sharma.

Cut-and-pasted gelatin silver prints, opaque watercolour and gold on paper; c. 1930s–1940s.
20 x 25 in. (50.8 x 63.5 cm).

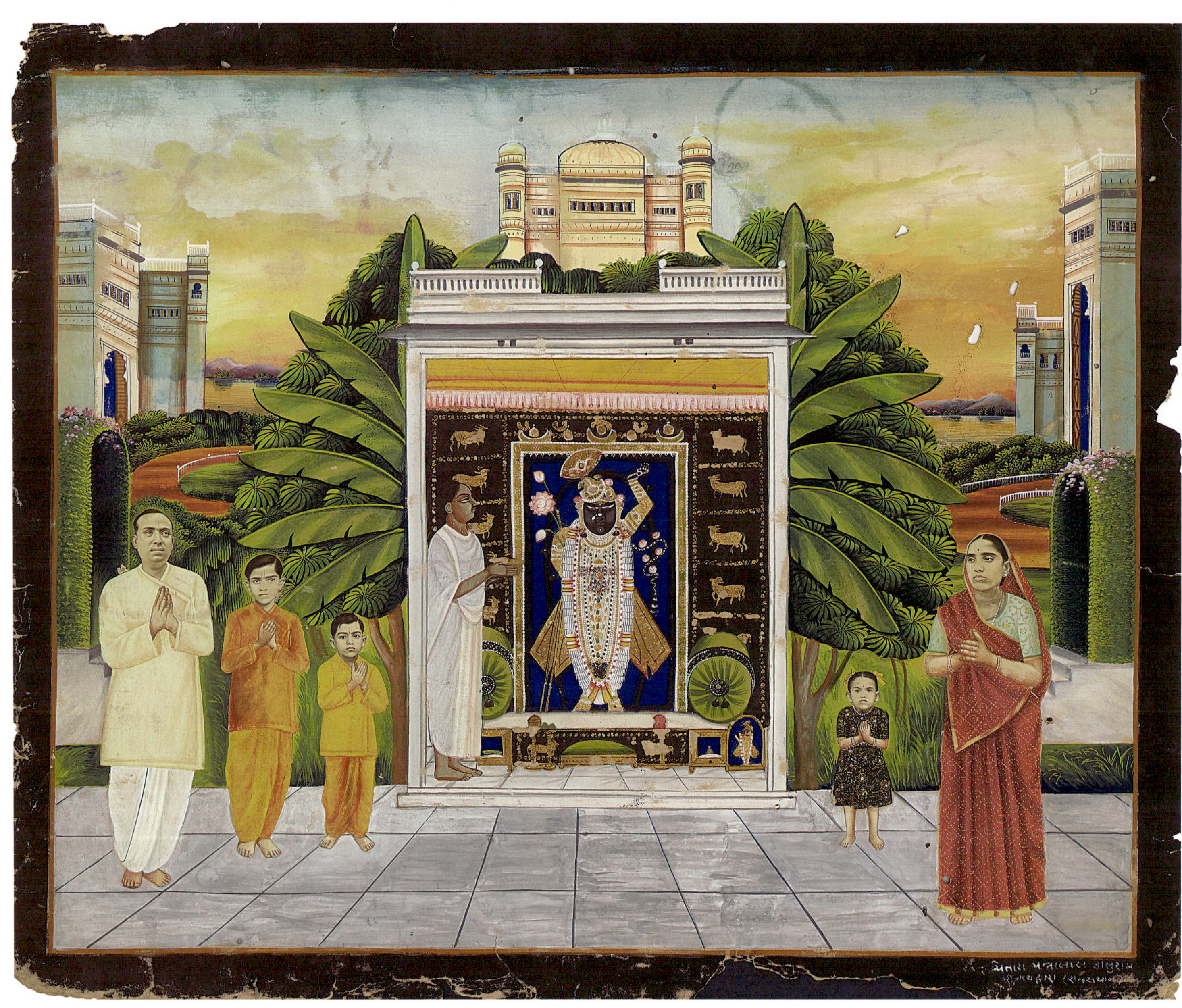

20. *Manorath* on the Occasion of Gopashtami.
Pannalal Kaluram.

Cut-and-pasted gelatin silver prints, opaque watercolour and gold on paper; c. 1940s. 19.8 x 23.5 in. (50.3 x 59.7 cm).

Inscribed in Gujarati on the recto: *cetārā pannālāl kālurām // śrīnāthdvārā (rājasthān)*

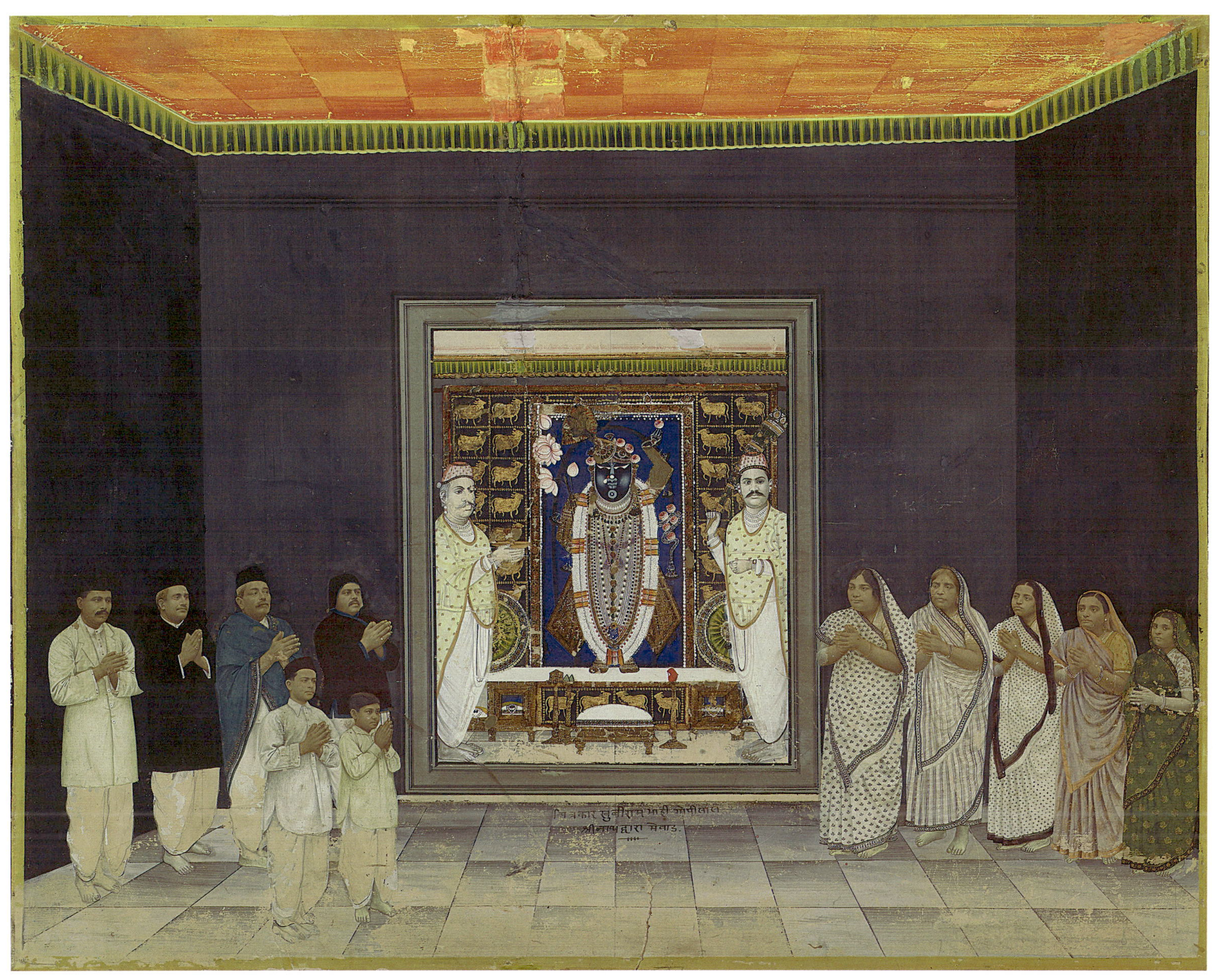

21. Family Attending the Gopashtami Celebrations Officiated by Govardhanlal and Damodarlal.
Khubiram and Gopilal.

Cut-and-pasted gelatin silver prints, opaque watercolour and gold on paper; c. 1940s.
22 x 27.5 in. (56 x 69.6 cm).

Inscribed in Hindi on the recto: *citrkār khubīrām bhāī gopīlāl // śrīnāthdvārā mevāḍ*

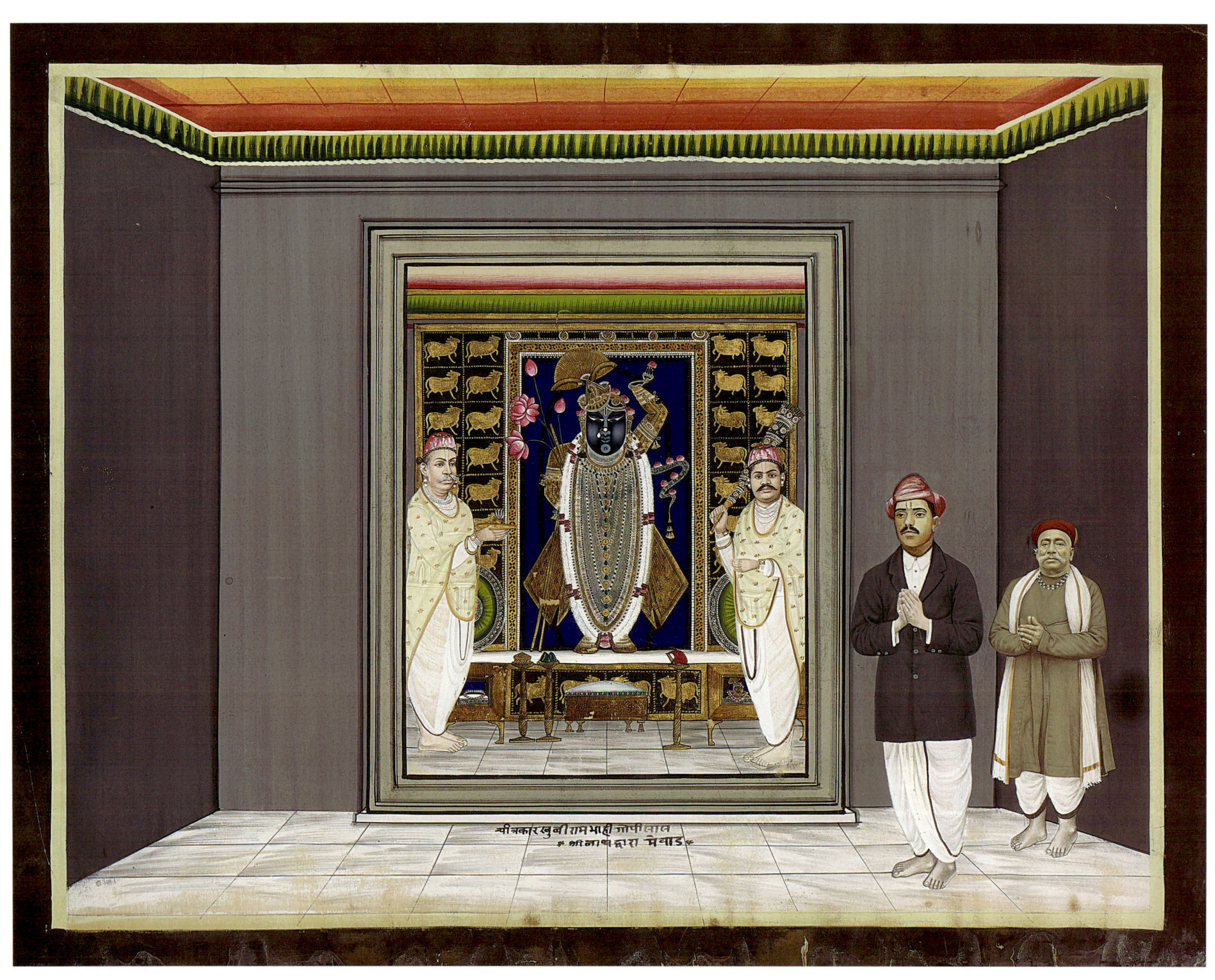

22. *Manorath* Performed by Govardhanlal and Damodarlal on the Occasion of Gopashtami.
Khubiram and Gopilal.

Cut-and-pasted gelatin silver prints, opaque watercolour and gold on paper; c. 1940s.
19.75 x 25 in. (50.2 x 63.5 cm).

Inscribed in Hindi on the recto: *citrkār khubīrām bhāhī gopīlāl // śrīnāthdvārā mevāḍ*

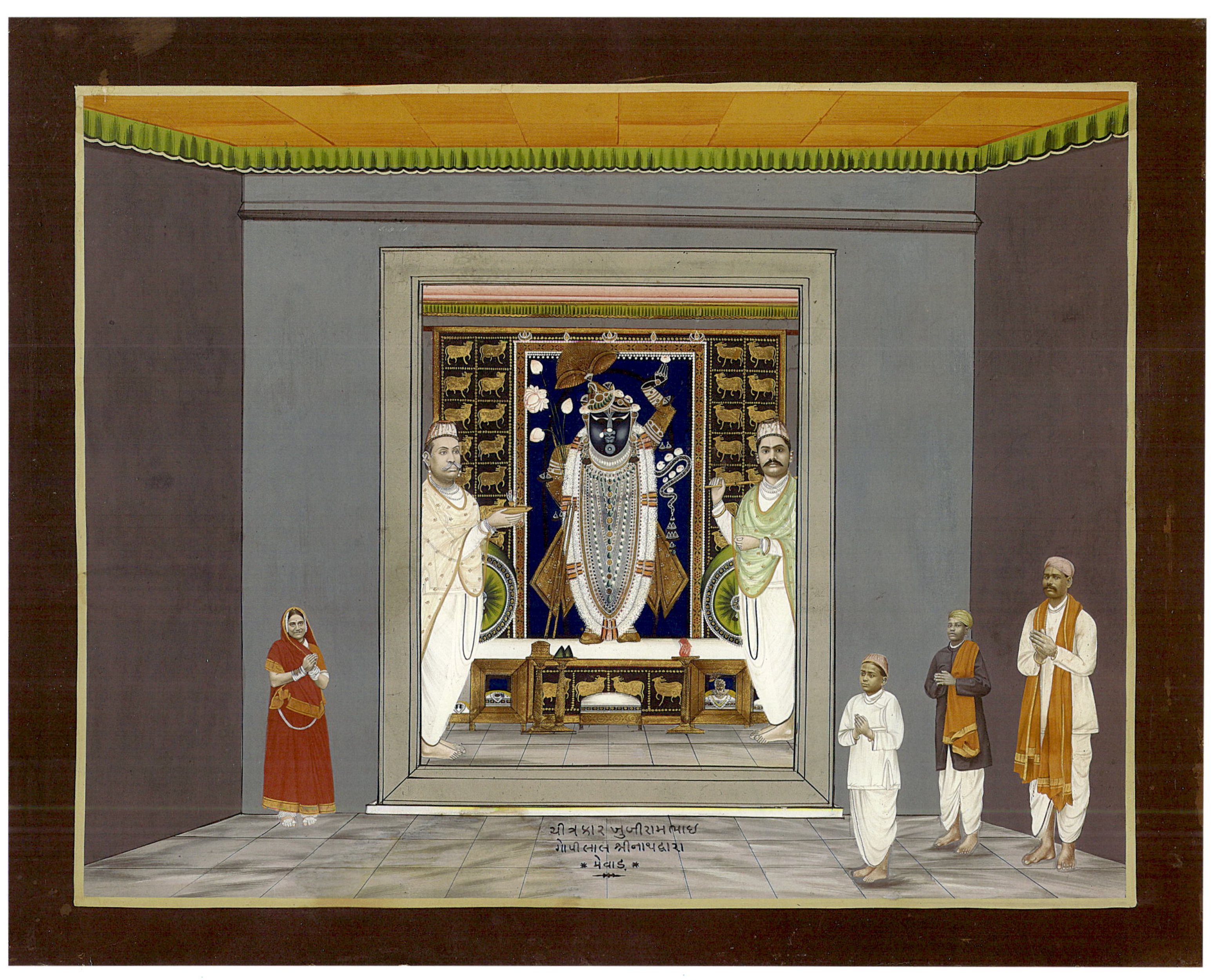

23. *Manorath* Performed by Govardhanlal and Damodarlal on the Occasion of Gopashtami.
Khubiram and Gopilal.

Cut-and-pasted gelatin silver prints, opaque watercolour and gold on paper; c. 1940s.
20 x 25 in (50.8 x 63.5 cm).

Inscribed in Gujarati on the recto: *cītrkār khubīrāmbhāi // gopīlāl śrīnāthdvārā // mevāḍ*

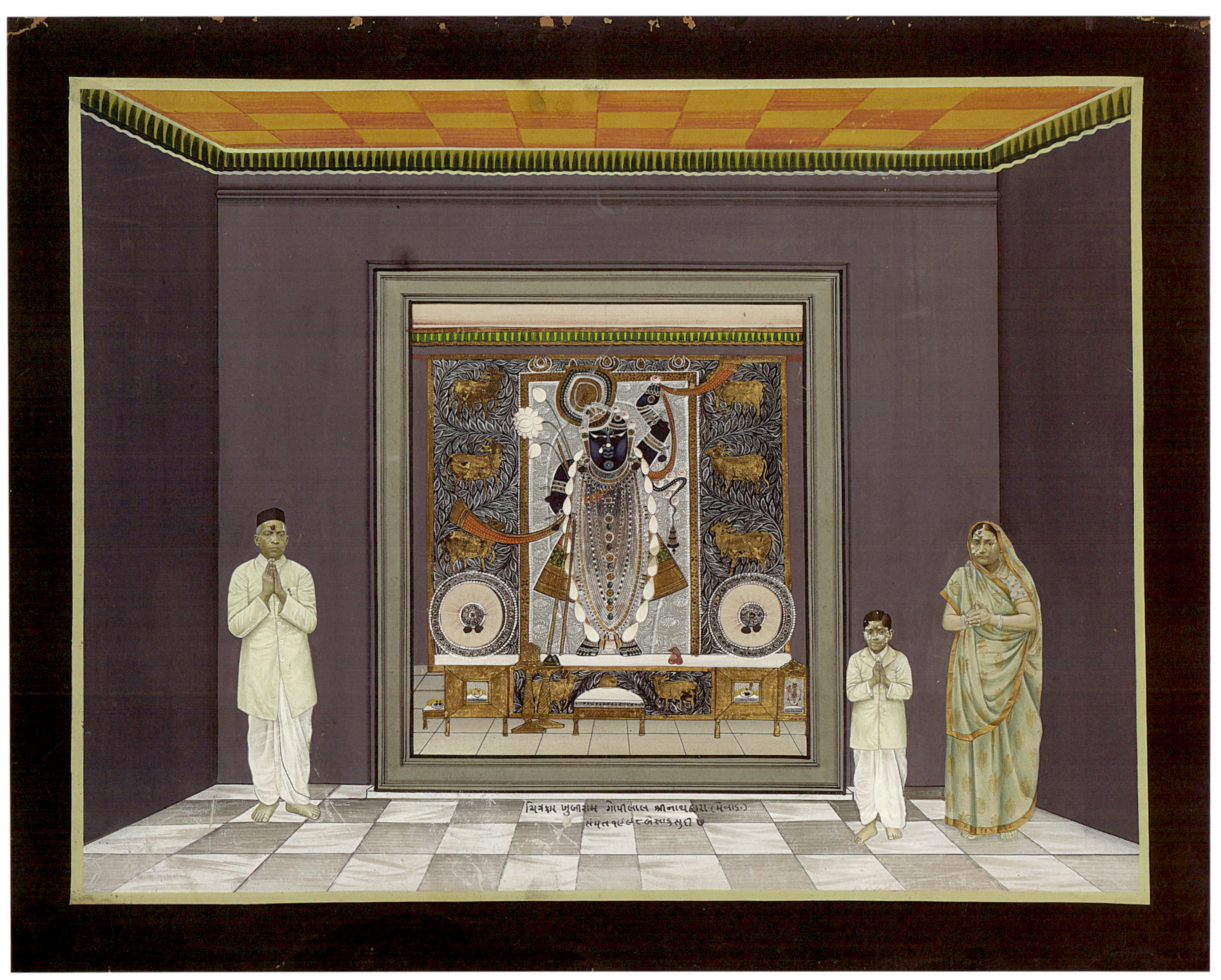

24. *Manorath* on the Occasion of Gopashtami.

Khubiram and Gopilal.

Cut-and-pasted gelatin silver prints, opaque watercolour and gold on paper; dated 1941 (VS 1998).
19.8 x 24.7 in. (50.2 x 62.7 cm).

Inscribed in Gujarati on the recto: *citrkār khubīrām gopīlāl śrīnāthdvārā (mevāḍ) // saṁmat 1998 besāk sudī 7*

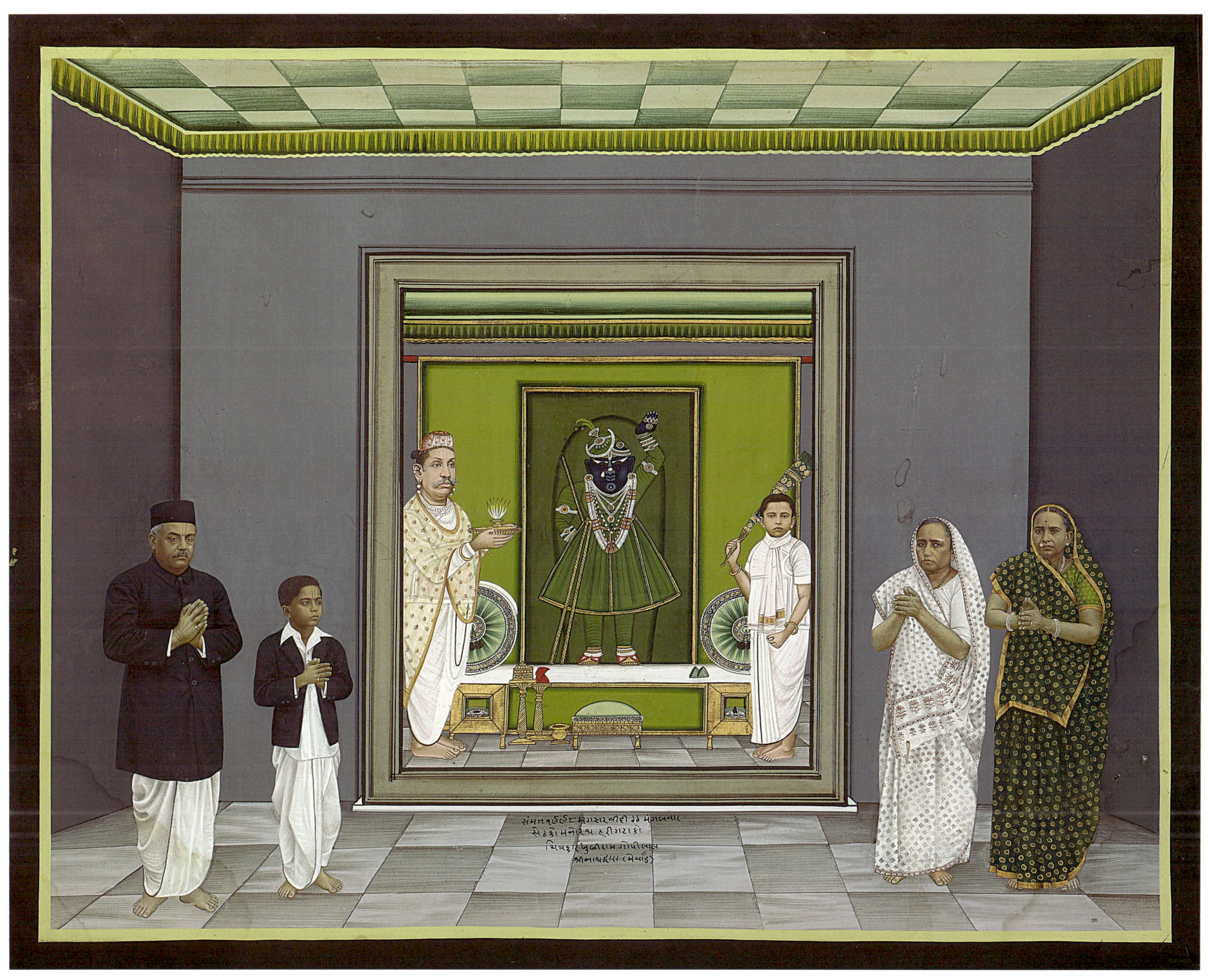

25. Family Attending a *Manorath* Performed by Govardhanlal and a Young Priest.
Khubiram and Gopilal.

Cut-and-pasted gelatin silver prints, opaque watercolour and gold on paper; dated 1941 (VS 1998).
19.9 x 23.8 in. (50.5 x 60.5 cm).

Inscribed in Gujarati on the recto: *saṁmat 1998 magsar vīdī 11 maṅgalvār // seṭh ko manorath harīgaṭāko // citrkār khubīrām gopīlāl // śrīnāthdvārā (mevāḍ)*

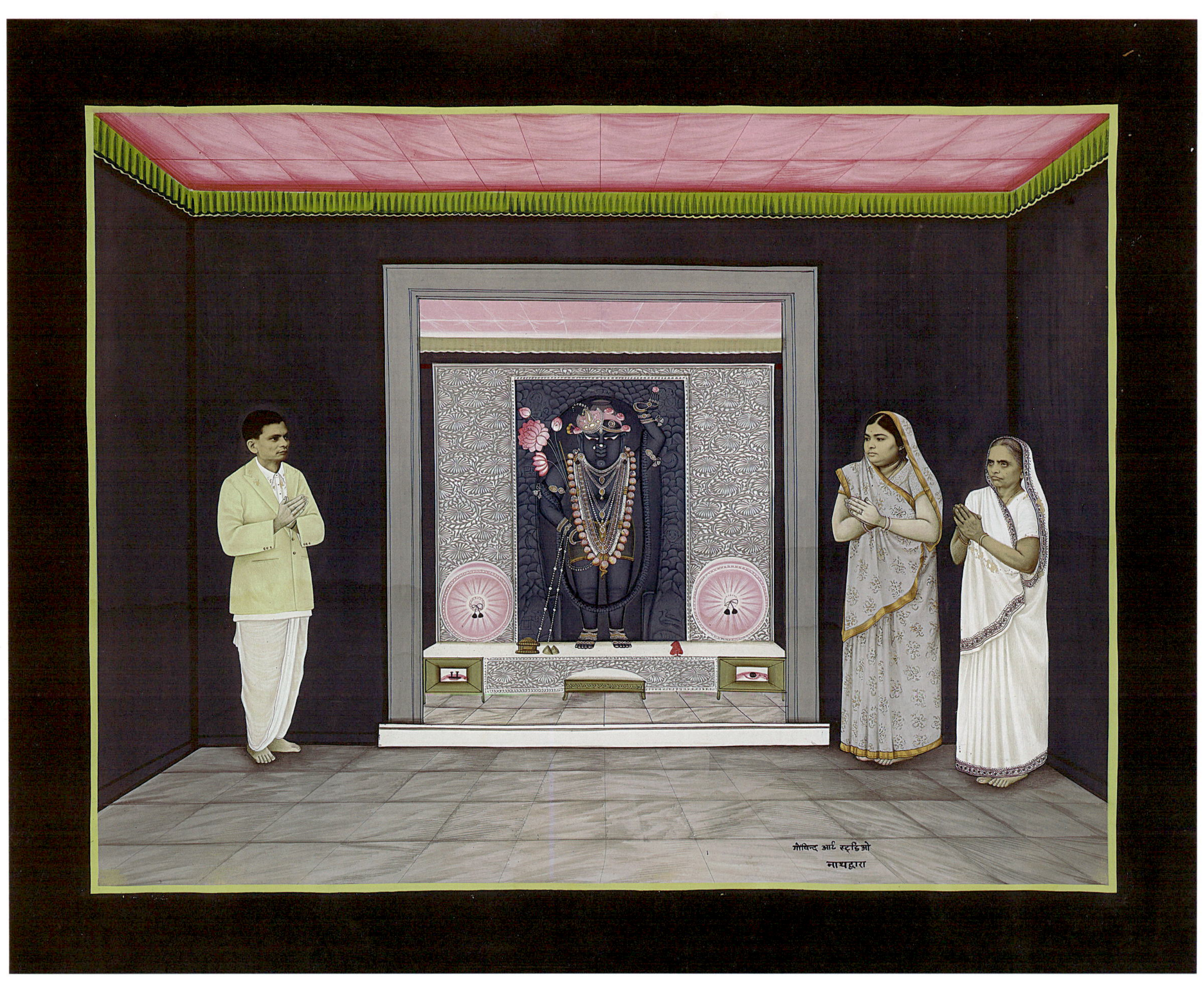

26. *Manorath* of Shrinathji on a Summer's Day.
Govind Art Studio, Nathdwara.

Cut-and-pasted gelatin silver prints, opaque watercolour and gold on paper; c. 1940s.
19.5 x 24 in. (49.5 x 61 cm).

Inscribed in Hindi on the recto: *govind art studio // nāthdvārā*

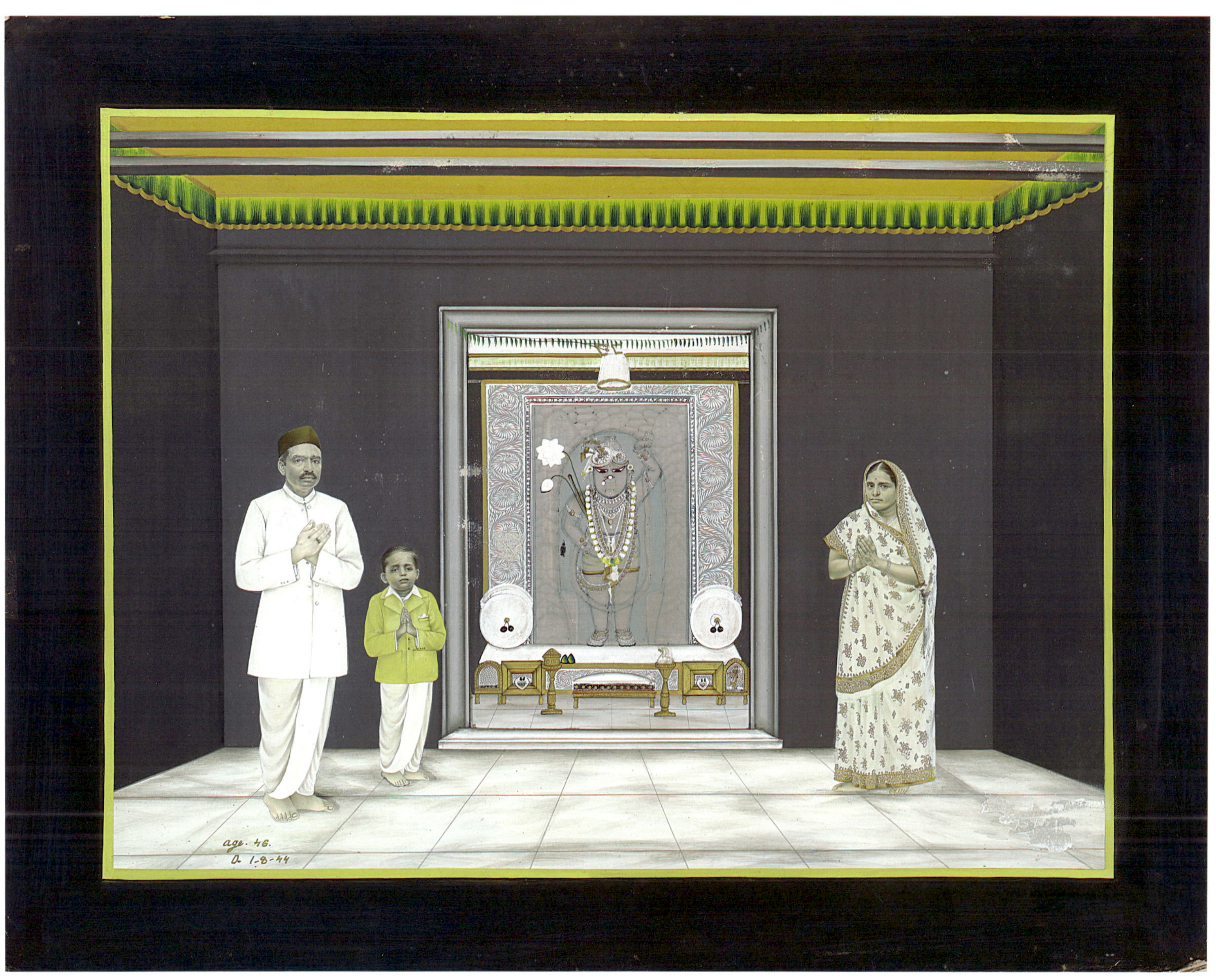

27. ***Manorath*** **of Shrinathji on a Summer's Day.**
Unknown artist or studio.

Cut-and-pasted gelatin silver prints, opaque watercolour and gold on paper; dated 1 August 1944.
19.9 x 24.9 in. (50.5 x 63.2 cm).

Inscribed in English on the recto: *age 46 // D. 1-8-44 // [obliterated inscription on the bottom right]*

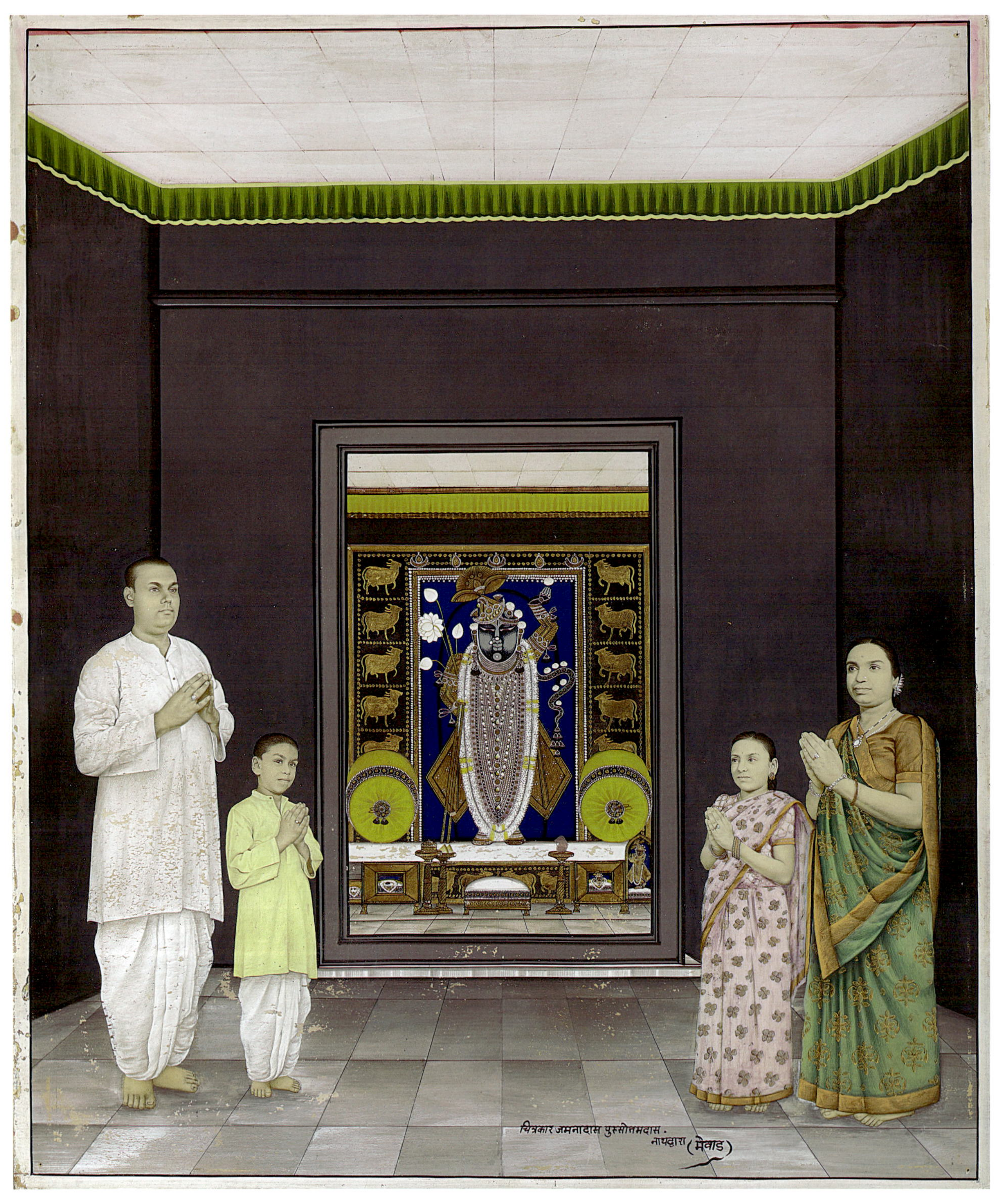

28. *Manorath* with a Family from Ahmedabad on the Occasion of Gopashtami.
Jamnadas Purusottamdas.

Cut-and-pasted gelatin silver prints, opaque watercolour and gold on paper; c. 1946.
28 x 20 in. (71.1 x 50.8 cm).

Inscribed in Hindi on the recto: *citrkār jamnādās purusottamdās // nāthdvārā (mevāḍ)*

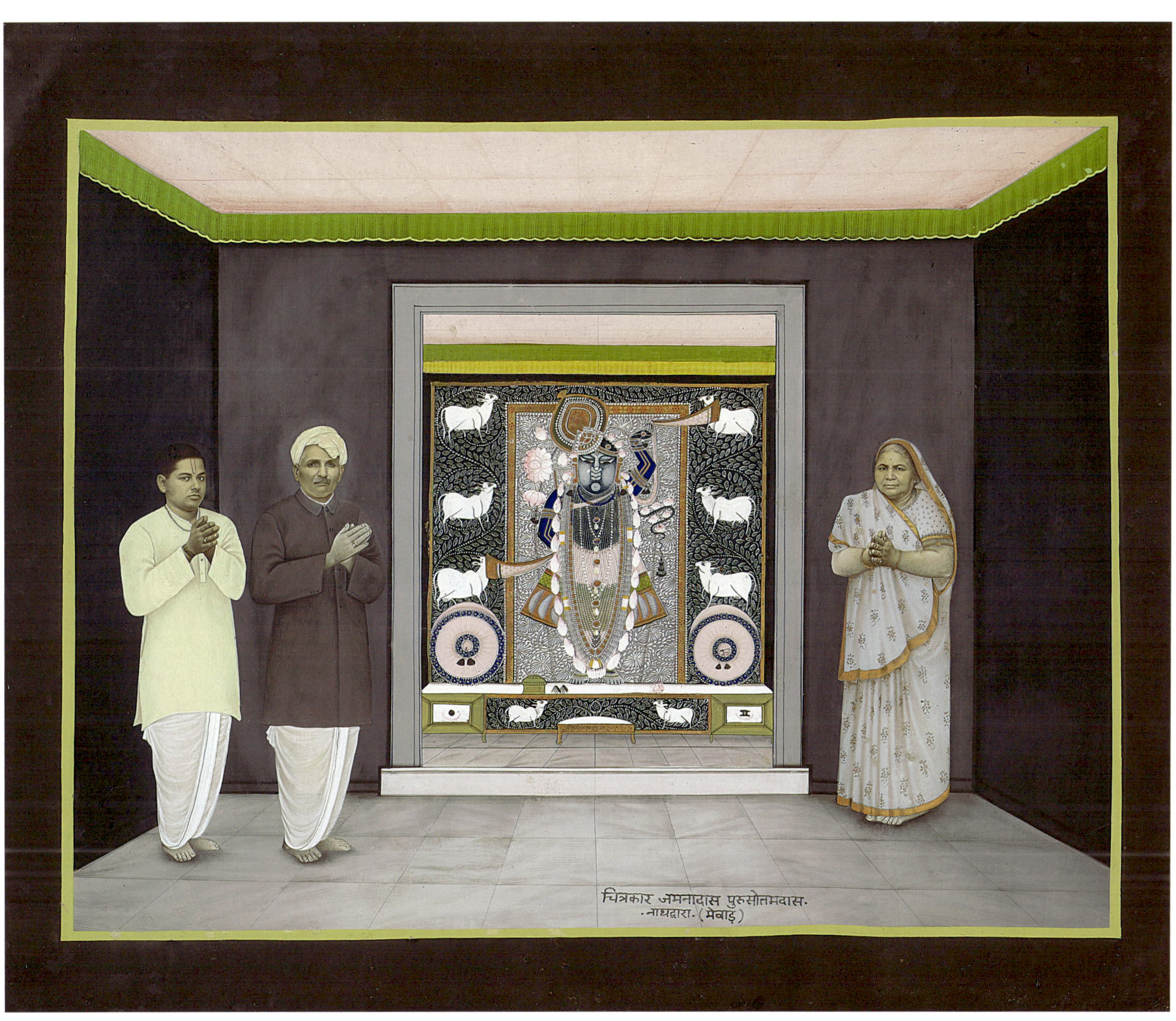

29. *Manorath* on the Occasion of Gopashtami.
Jamnadas Purusottamdas.

Cut-and-pasted gelatin silver prints, opaque watercolour and gold on paper; c. 1940s.
20.1 x 23.6 in (51 x 60 cm).

Inscribed in Hindi on the recto: *citrkār jamnādās purusottamdās // nāthdvārā (mevāḍ)*

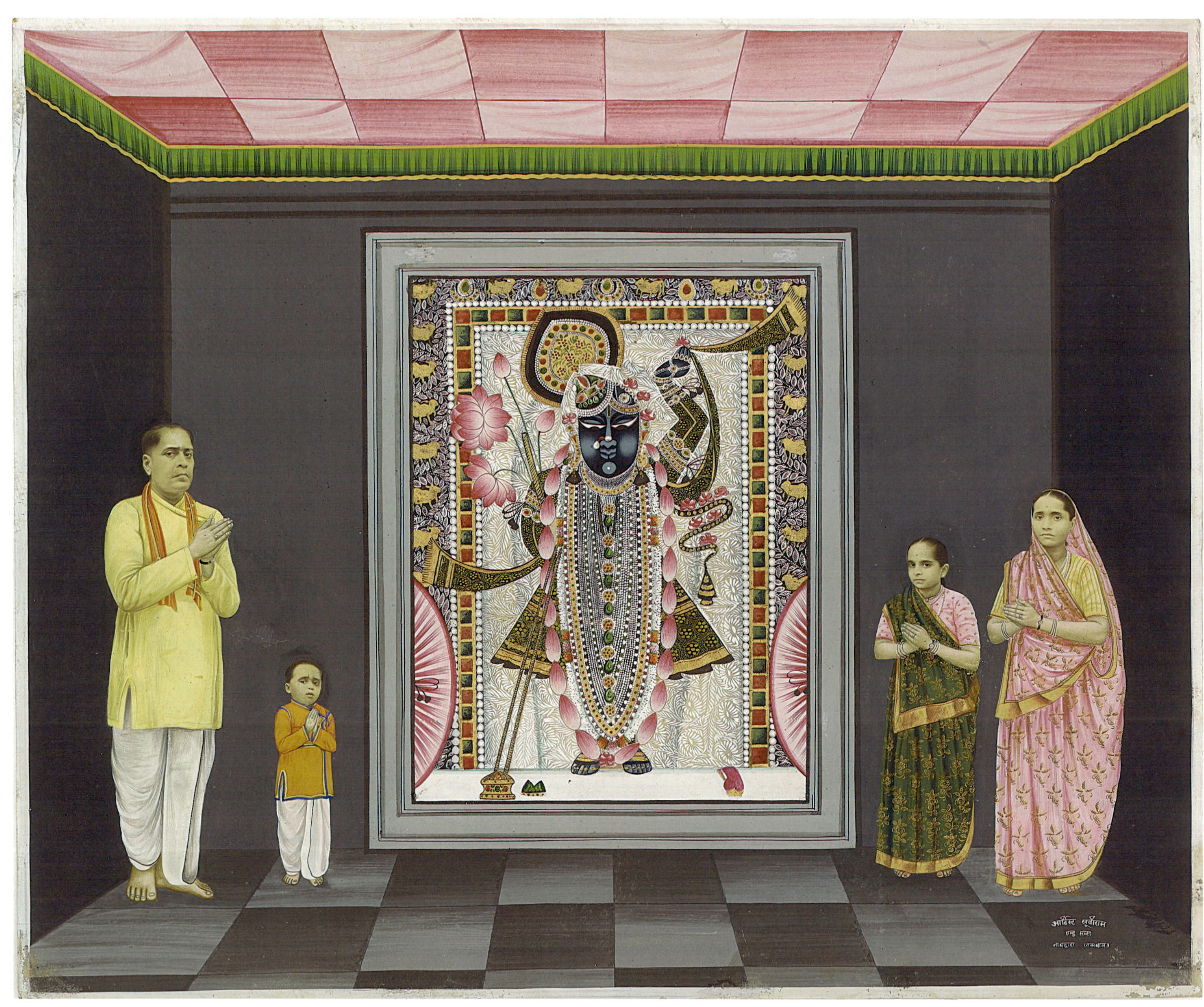

30. *Manorath* of Shrinathji.

Artist Khubiram and Sons.

Cut-and-pasted gelatin silver prints, opaque watercolour and gold on paper; c. 1950s.
19.7 x 23.6 in (50 x 60 cm).

Inscribed in Hindi on the recto: *artist khūbīrām // eṇḍ sans // nāthdvārā (rājasthān)*

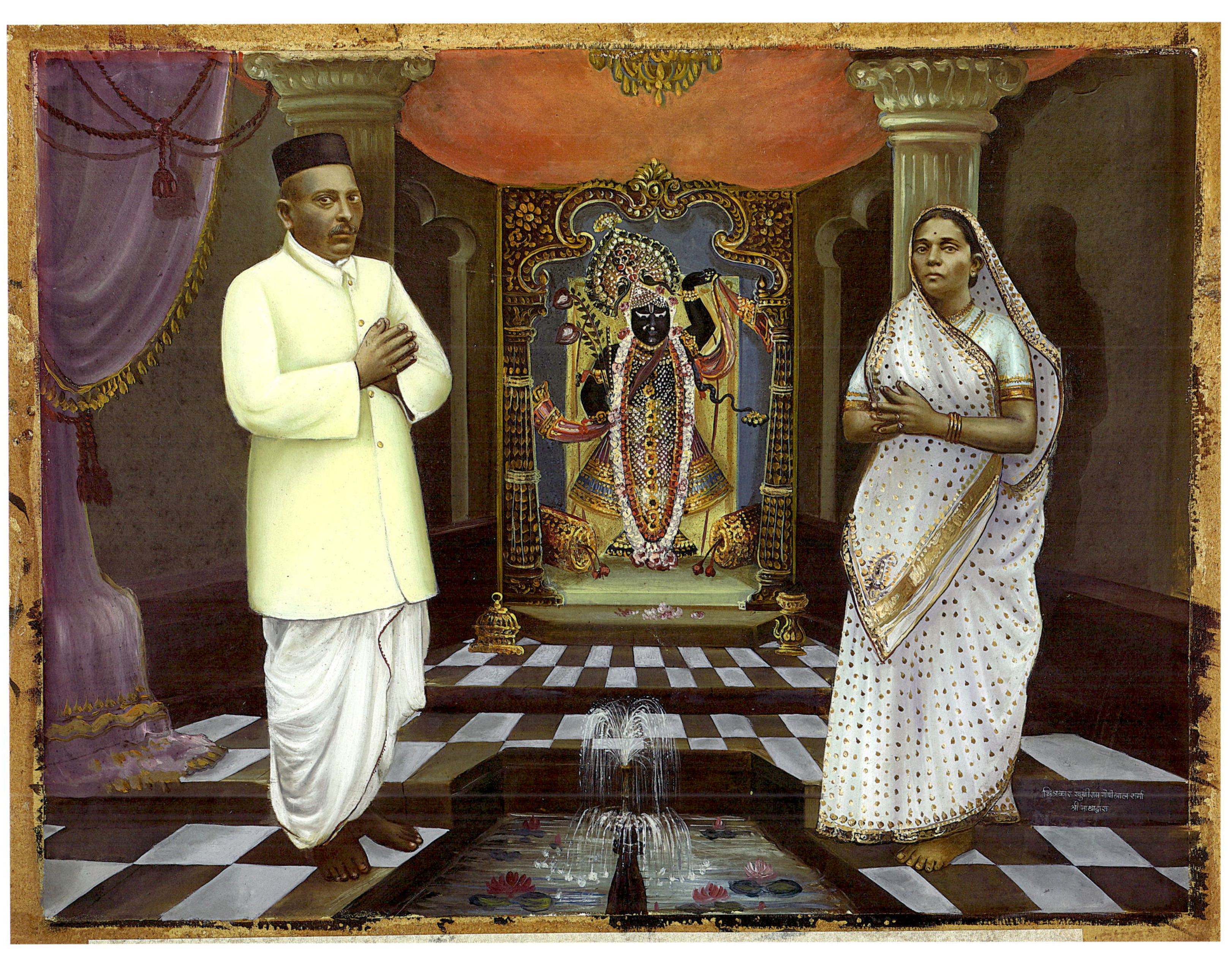

31. *Manorath* with a Couple in the Temple of Shrinathji.
Khubiram and Gopilal.

Oil paint on gelatin silver print; c. 1930s.
20.5 x 26.2 in. (52.1 x 66.5 cm).

Inscribed in Hindi on the recto: *citrkār khubīrām gopīlāl śarmā // śrī nāthādvār*

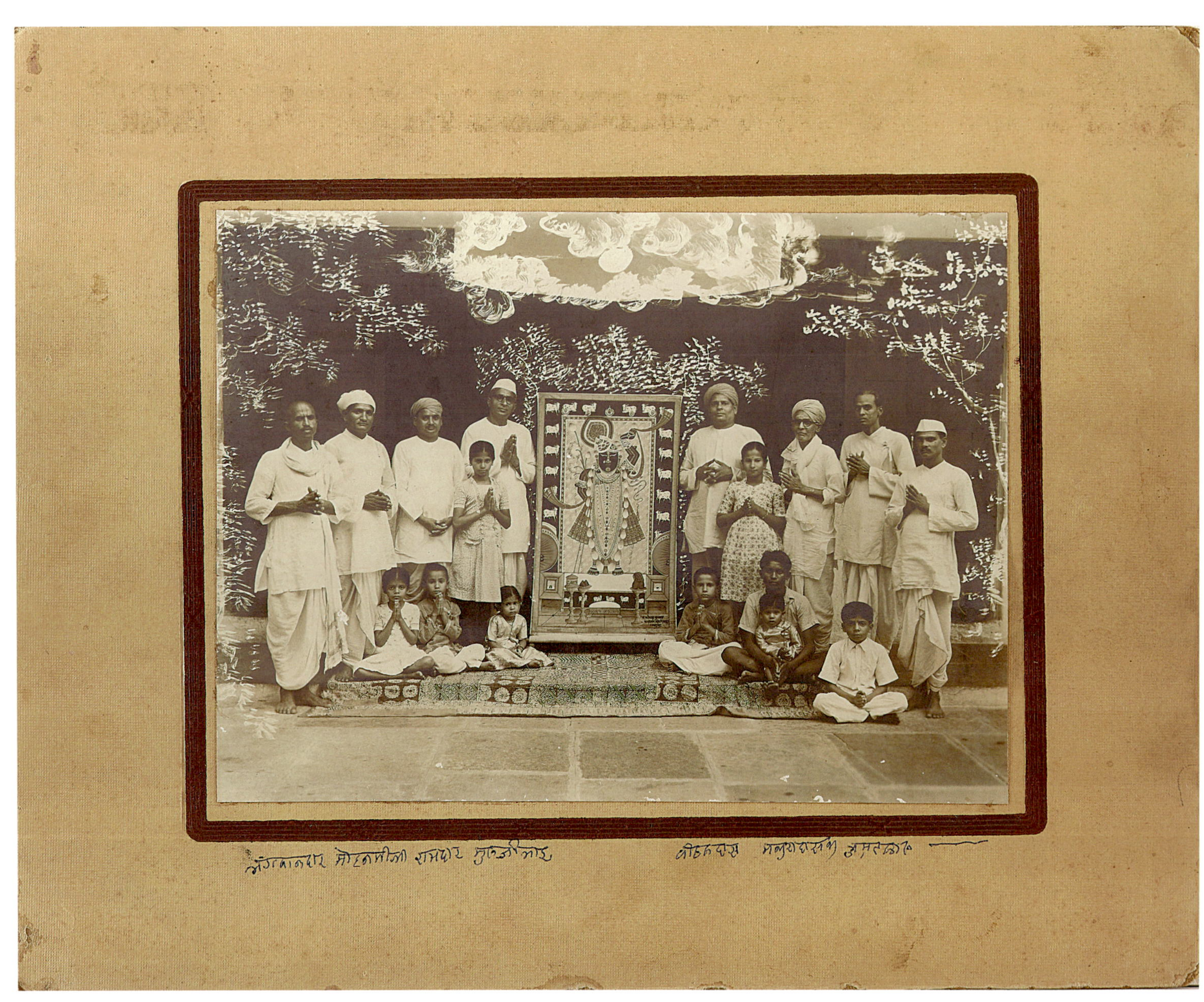

32. Group Photograph with Devotees Next to a *Pichhwai* of Shrinathji.
Narendra Kumar Paliwal.

Gelatin silver print; c. 1950s.
Photograph with mount: 9.75 x 12 in. (24.8 x 30.5 cm).

Inscribed in Hindi. On the photograph (bottom right of the *pichhwai*): *pań. narendra kumār // pālīvāl photographar // nāthdvārā*
On the mount: *bhagvāndār mohanmiśrī rāmdār muljībhāī / viṭhaldās mathurādāsji amṛt* ... [illegible]

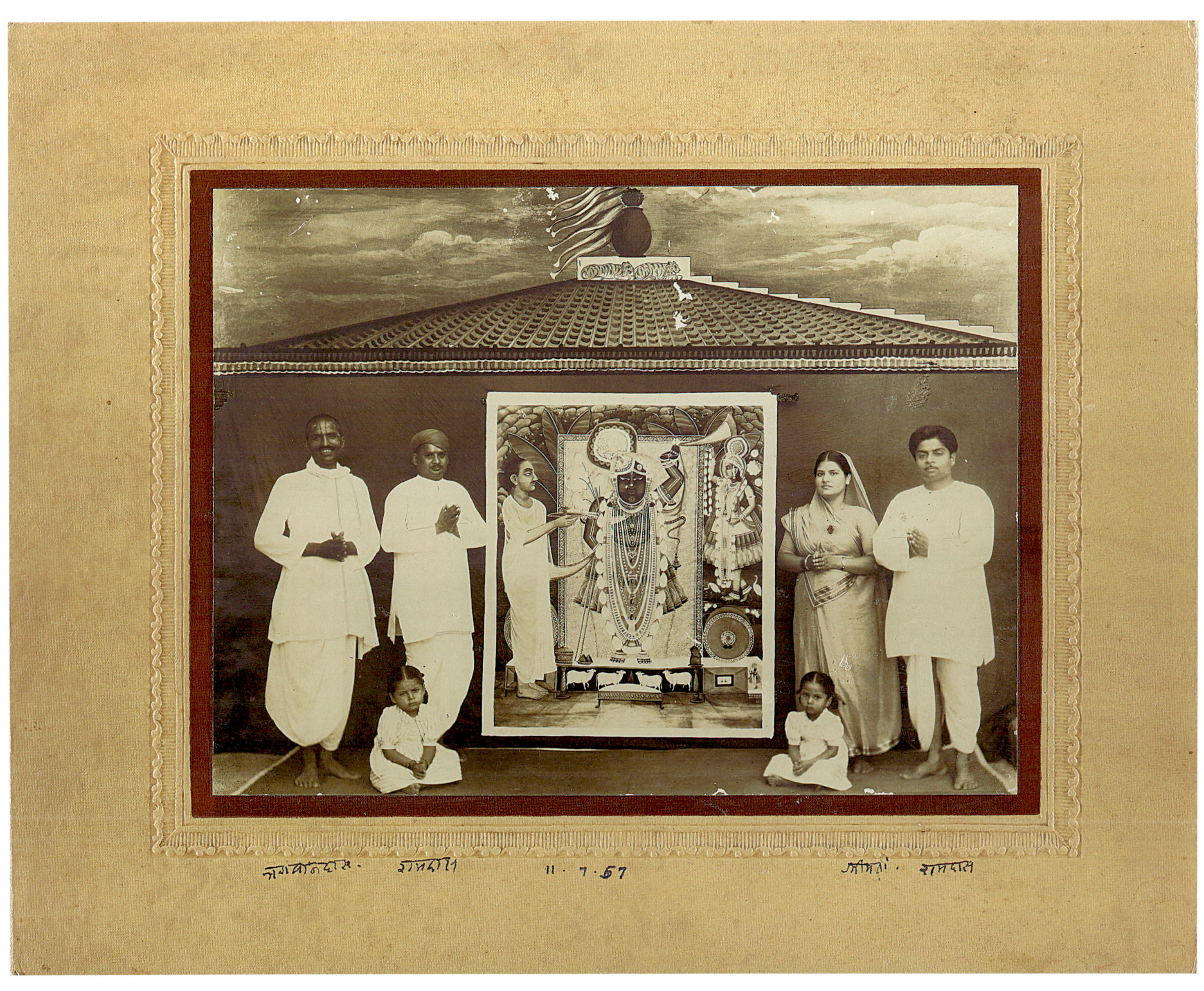

33. Photographic *Manorath*.
Unknown photographer or studio.
Gelatin silver print; dated 11 July 1957.
Photograph with mount: 9.5 x 11.75 in. (24.1 x 29.8 cm).
Inscribed in Hindi on the mount: *bhagvāndās rāmdās / 11.7.57 / śrīmatī rāmdās*

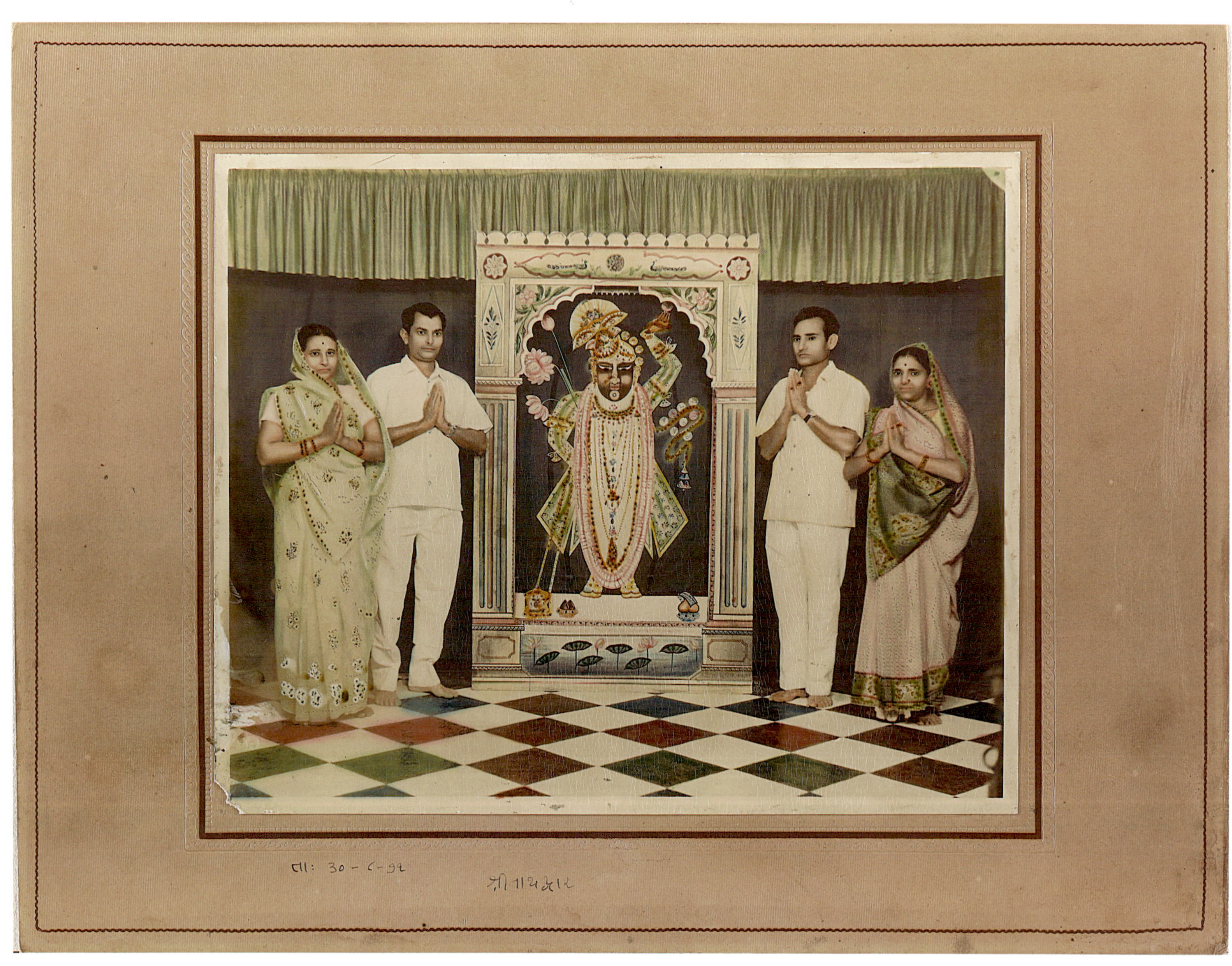

34. Photographic *Manorath*.
Unknown photographer or studio.
Watercolour on gelatin silver print; dated 30 August 1971.
Photograph with mount: 13.7 x 17.7 in. (34.8 x 45 cm).
Inscribed in Hindi on the mount: *tā: 30-8-71* // *śrīnāthdvār*

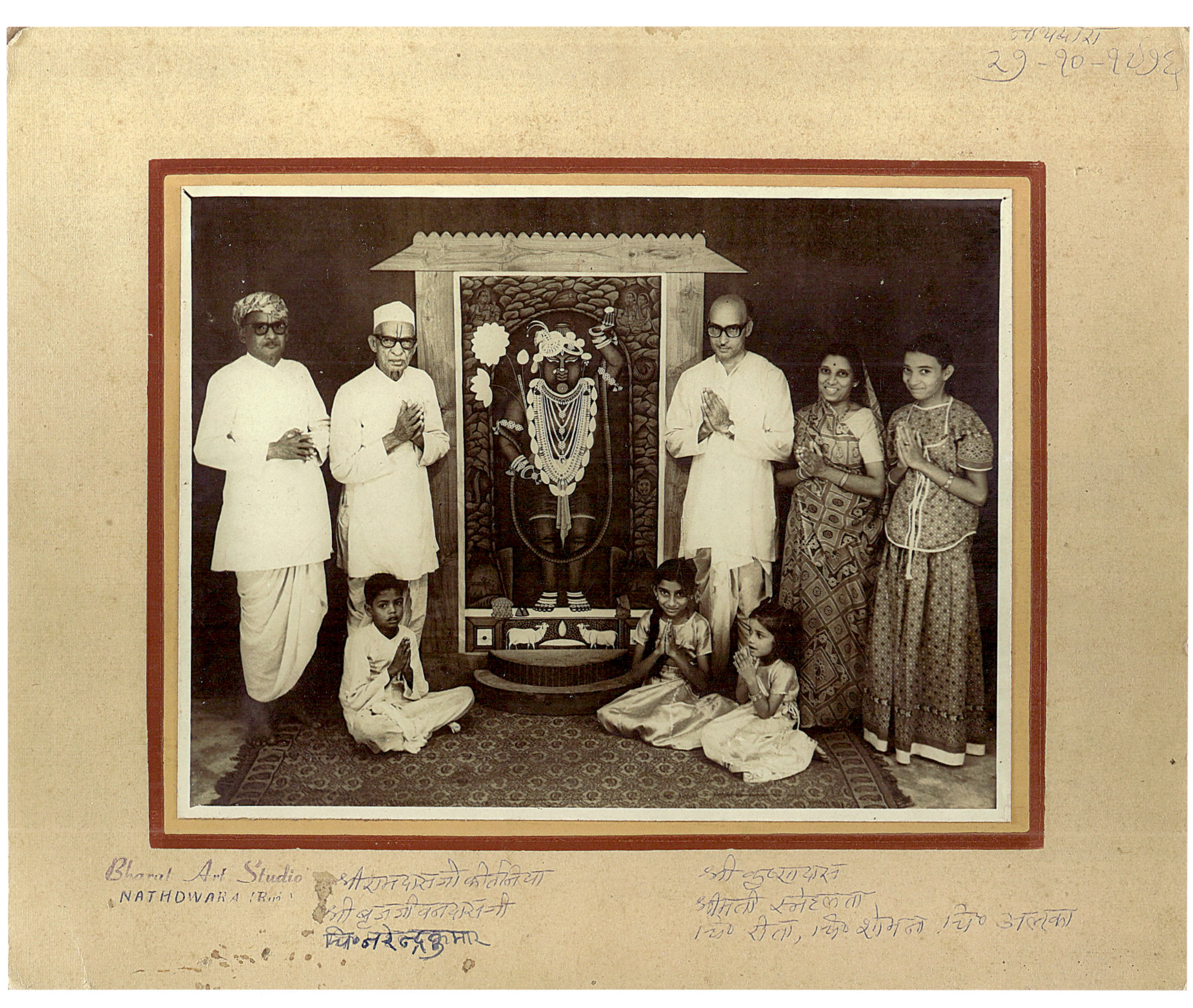

35. Photographic *Manorath*.
Bharat Art Studio, Nathdwara.

Gelatin silver print; dated 27 October 1976.
Photograph with mount: 9.6 x 11.75 in. (24.4 x 29.8 cm).

Inscribed on the mount. In Hindi on the top right: *nāthdvārā // 27-10-1976*
Rubber-stamped on the bottom left: *Bharat Art Studio // Nathdwara (Raj.)*
In Hindi, group of names on the left (top to bottom): *śrīrāmdāsjī kīrtaniyā // śrībrjjīvandāsjī // ci. narendrkumār*
Group of names on the right (top to bottom): *śrīkṛṣṇadās // śrīmatī snehlatā // ci. rītā, ci. śobhnā ci. alkā*

Glossary

Goswami: *(gosvāmī)* a priest of the Pushti Marg sect. See also ***tilkayat***.

Govardhanlal: (Govardhanlāl, 1862–1934) important Pushti Marg personality and patron of the arts. He was appointed as the *tilkayat*, or head priest, of the Shrinathji temple at a very young age in 1876. He is known to have promoted numerous projects and religious events to relaunch Nathdwara as a devotional centre. In 1908 he organized the Festival of the Five *Svarup*s.

Navnitpriyaji: (Navnītpriyjī) small metal icon in the form of Krishna as a child holding a ball of butter in one hand. This *svarup* resides at the *haveli* temple of Nathdwara.

Pichhwai: *(pichvāī)* temple hanging used in Pushti Marg rituals. The *pichhwai*s used in the Nathdwara temple have specific measures, which are reported by Amit Ambalal to be approximately three meters in length by 1.8 meters in height. They can be made of different types of materials, such as cotton and silk, and they can be decorated in a variety of ways and techniques.

Pushti Marg: (Puṣṭi Mārg or Puṣṭimārg) translated as "Path of Grace," this is a Krishnaite devotional sect that was founded at the beginning of the sixteenth century by the philosopher Vallabhacharya (1479–1531). It is also known as Vallabha Sampradaya, after its founder's name, and it promotes the householder way of life *(grhastha)*, and a selfless devotion to Krishna.

Shrinathji: (Śrī Nāthjī) black marble sculpture said to measure 1.37 meters. It has its left arm raised in the act of lifting Mount Govardhan. Shrinathji is the primary icon, or *svarup*, of Pushti Marg, and it is installed in the *haveli* temple of Nathdwara. The icon is known to have miraculously manifested itself to Vallabhacharya on Mount Govardhan in 1492.

Svarup: *(svarūp)* self-manifested icon. This term indicates a statue of divine nature which is, therefore, different from a *murti*, or man-made sculpture. Pushti Marg recognizes nine such *svarup*s, which are also known by the name of *navnidhi*s (the nine treasures). These icons are said to have miraculously appeared to Vallabhacharya or one of his first disciples during the foundational years of the sect. They are: Shrinathji and Navnitpriyaji residing in the *haveli* temple of Nathdwara, Dwarkadishji of Kankroli, Mathureshji of Kota, Vitthalnathji of Nathdwara, Madanmohanji and Gokulcandramaji of Kaman, Gokulnathji of Gokul, and Balkrishnaji of Surat.

Tilkayat: *(tilkāyat)* title of the head priest of the Shrinathji temple of Nathdwara.

List of Artists and Studios

Artists

- Ambalal Khemraj: Cat. no. 3.
- Bhuralal Motilalnath Sharma (b. 1899): Cat. no. 19 (attributed); Fig. 15.
- Champalal Hiralal Gaur (c. 1875–1930): Cat. no. 5; Fig. 6.
- Ghasiram Hardev Sharma (1868–1930): Cat. nos. 1, 7; Fig. 3.
- Gopilal Govardhanlal Sharma (1890–1970): see Khubiram and Gopilal.
- Jamnadas Purusottamdas: Cat. nos. 28–29.
- Kanhaiyalal Bhimraj: Cat. no. 8.
- Khubiram Nathuji Sharma (1880–1966): see Khubiram and Gopilal; and Artist Khubiram and Sons.
- Narendra Kumar Paliwal (photographer): Cat. no. 32.
- Nathalal Jaikrishnadas: Cat. no. 4.
- Pannalal Kaluram: Cat. no. 20.
- Raghunath (also Rugnath) Sukhdev (1882–1924), son of Sukhdev Kishandas: Cat. no. 2; Fig. 8a (attributed).
- Sukhdev Kishandas (1853–1925): Fig. 7a.
- Udairam Bhagvandas: Cat. no. 6.

Studios

- Bharat Art Studio, Nathdwara: Cat. nos. 18, 35.
- Govind Art Studio, Nathdwara: Cat. no. 26.
- Khubiram and Gopilal (1907–c. late 1940s): Cat. nos. 11, 14–17, 21–25, 31; Figs. 8a, 16.
- Artist Khubiram and Sons (c. late 1940s–present): Cat. no. 30.

Cited Works

Agarvwal, Shalvi. *The Indian Portrait – VII: Trans-culturalisation of Lens and Brush through Painted Photographs.* Archer, 2015.

Aitken, Molly Emma. "Colonial-Period Court Painting and the Case of Bikaner." *Archives of Asian Art,* vol. 67, no. 1, April 2017, pp. 25–59.

Allana, Rahaab and Pramod Kumar K.G. *Painted Photographs: Coloured Portraiture in India.* Mapin Publishing and The Alkazi Collection of Photography, 2008.

Ambalal, Amit. *Krishna as Shrinathji. Rajasthani Paintings from Nathdvara.* Mapin Publishing, 1995.

——"*Manoratha* Paintings from Nathdwara." *Indian Painting: Themes, Histories, Interpretations. Essays in Honour of B. N. Goswamy,* edited by Mahesh Sharma and Padma Kaimal, Mapin Publishing, 2014, pp. 214–219.

——"The Tilkayats as Patrons: History and Painting in Nathdwara." *Gates of the Lord: The Tradition of Krishna Paintings,* edited by Madhuvanti Ghose, Mapin Publishing/The Art Institute of Chicago, 2015, pp. 26–35.

Barz, Richard. *The Bhakti Sect of Vallabhacarya.* Munshiram Manoharlal, 1992.

Dallapiccola, Anna, et.al. *Thanjavur's Gilded Gods: South Indian Paintings in the Kuldip Singh Collection.* Marg, 2018.

Dewan, Deepali. *Embellished Reality. Indian Painted Photographs: Towards a Transcultural History of Photography.* Royal Ontario Museum Press, 2012.

——"A Tale of Two Mediums: Paint and Photography in Udaipur." *A Magic World: New Visions of Indian Painting,* edited by Molly Emma Aitken, Marg, 2016, pp. 64–73

Eshaghi, Peyman. "To Capture a Cherished Past: Pilgrimage Photography at Imam Riza's Shrine, Iran." *Middle East Journal of Culture and Communication,* vol. 8, 2015, pp. 282–306.

Gaston, Anne-Marie. *Krishna's Musicians: Musicians and Music Making in the Temples of Nathdvara, Rajasthan.* Manohar, 1997.

Ghose, Madhuvanti, editor. *Gates of the Lord: The Tradition of Krishna Paintings.* Mapin Publishing/The Art Institute of Chicago, 2015.

Goswamy, B.N., and Karuna Goswamy. *Wondrous Images: Krishna Seen as Shrinath-Ji. Pichhwais of the Vallabha Sampradaya.* Sarabhai Foundation, 2014.

Jain, Jyotindra. *Indian Popular Culture: "The Conquest of the World as Picture."* Apeejay Press, 2004.

Jain, Kajri. *Gods in the Bazaar: The Economies of Indian Calendar Art.* Duke, 2007.

Jindel, Rajendra. *Culture of a Sacred Town: A Sociological Study of Nathdwara.* Popular Prakashan, 1976.

Krishna, Kalyan and Kay Talwar. *In Adoration of Krishna: Pichhwais of Shrinathji, Tapi Collection.* Garden Silk Mills Limited, 2007.

Lyons, Tryna. *The Artists of Nathadwara: The Practice of Painting in Rajasthan.* Mapin Publishing, 2004.

McGregor, Ronald Stuart. *The Oxford Hindi-English Dictionary.* Oxford University Press, 1993.

Mitter, Partha. "The Dawn of Photography in India: A Complex Legacy of the Photographic Studio." *The Artful Pose: Early Studio Photography in Mumbai c. 1855–1940,* Mapin Publishing, 2010, pp. 9–25.

Monier-Williams, Monier. *Sanskrit-English Dictionary.* Munshiram Manoharlal, 1994.

Mulji, Karsandas. *History of the Sect of the Maharajas, or Vallabhacharyas, in Western India.* Trübner and Co., 1865.

Nanda, Vivek. *Krishna & Devotion: Temple Hangings from Western India.* Asia House, 2009.

Nardi, Isabella. "Portraiture and Politics: Royal and Devotional Allegiances in the Paintings of the Garh Mahal, Jhalawar." *South Asian Studies,* 2017, DOI: 10.1080/02666030.2017.1409937.

——"La Miniatura come Documento Storico: Le Celebrazioni di Saptasvarupa Annakutotsava al Tempio di Śrī Nāthjī a Nathdwara nel 1822." *Annali Sezione Orientale,* vol. 77, 2017, pp. 215–232, DOI: 10.1163/24685631-12340031.

——"*Manorath* of Śrī Nāthjī: Evoking the *Alaukika* in an Early Twentieth Century Painting from Nathdwara." *South Asian Archaeology and Art: Research Presented at the 23rd Conference of the European Association for South Asian Archaeology and Art, Cardiff, 2016,* edited by Laxshmi Greaves Andrade and Adam Hardy, vol. 2, Dev Publishers, 2019.

Pauwels, Heidi, and Emilia Bachrach. "Aurangzeb as Iconoclast? Vaishnava Accounts of the Krishna Images' Exodus from Braj." *Journal of the Royal Asiatic Society*, vol. 28, no. 3, 2018, pp. 485–508.

Peabody, Norbert. *Hindu Kingship and Polity in Precolonial India*. Cambridge University Press, 2003.

Pinney, Christopher. *Photos of the Gods: The Printed Image and Political Struggle in India.* Oxford University Press, 2004.

——"Stirred by Photography." *Allegory and Illusion: Early Portrait Photography from South Asia,* edited by Christopher Pinney, et. al., Mapin Publishing and The Alkazi Collection of Photography, 2013, pp. 12–29.

Relia, Anil. *The Indian Portrait – II: Sacred Journey of Tilkayat Govardhanlalji (1862–1934), Nathdwara.* Archer, 2013.

Robbins, Kenneth X and Marvin Tokayer, editors. *Jews and the Indian National Art Project.* Niyogi Books, 2015.

Ruia, Aditya. "Nathdwara: Photography as Propaganda." *Academia.edu,* www.academia.edu/37148479/Nathdwara_Photography_as_Propaganda. Accessed 7 September 2018.

Saha, Shandip. "The Darbār, the British, and the Runaway Mahārāja: Religion and Politics in Nineteenth-Century Western India." *South Asia Research*, vol. 27, no. 3, 2007, pp. 271–91.

Shah, Anita B. "Devotion and Patronage: The Story of a Pushtimarg Family." *Gates of the Lord: The Tradition of Krishna Paintings,* edited by Madhuvanti Ghose, Mapin Publishing/The Art Institute of Chicago, 2015, pp. 42–53.

Skelton, Robert. *Rajasthani Temple Hangings of the Krishna Cult from the Collection of Karl Mann.* American Federation of the Arts, 1973.

Toomey, Paul M. "Krishna's Consuming Passions: Food as Metaphor and Metonym for Emotion at Mount Govardhan." *Divine Passions: The Social Construction of Emotion in India,* edited by Owen M. Lynch, University of California Press, 1990, pp. 157–182.

Vaudeville, Charlotte. "The Govardhan Myth in Northern India." *Indo-Iranian Journal,* vol. 22, no. 1, 1980, pp. 1–45.

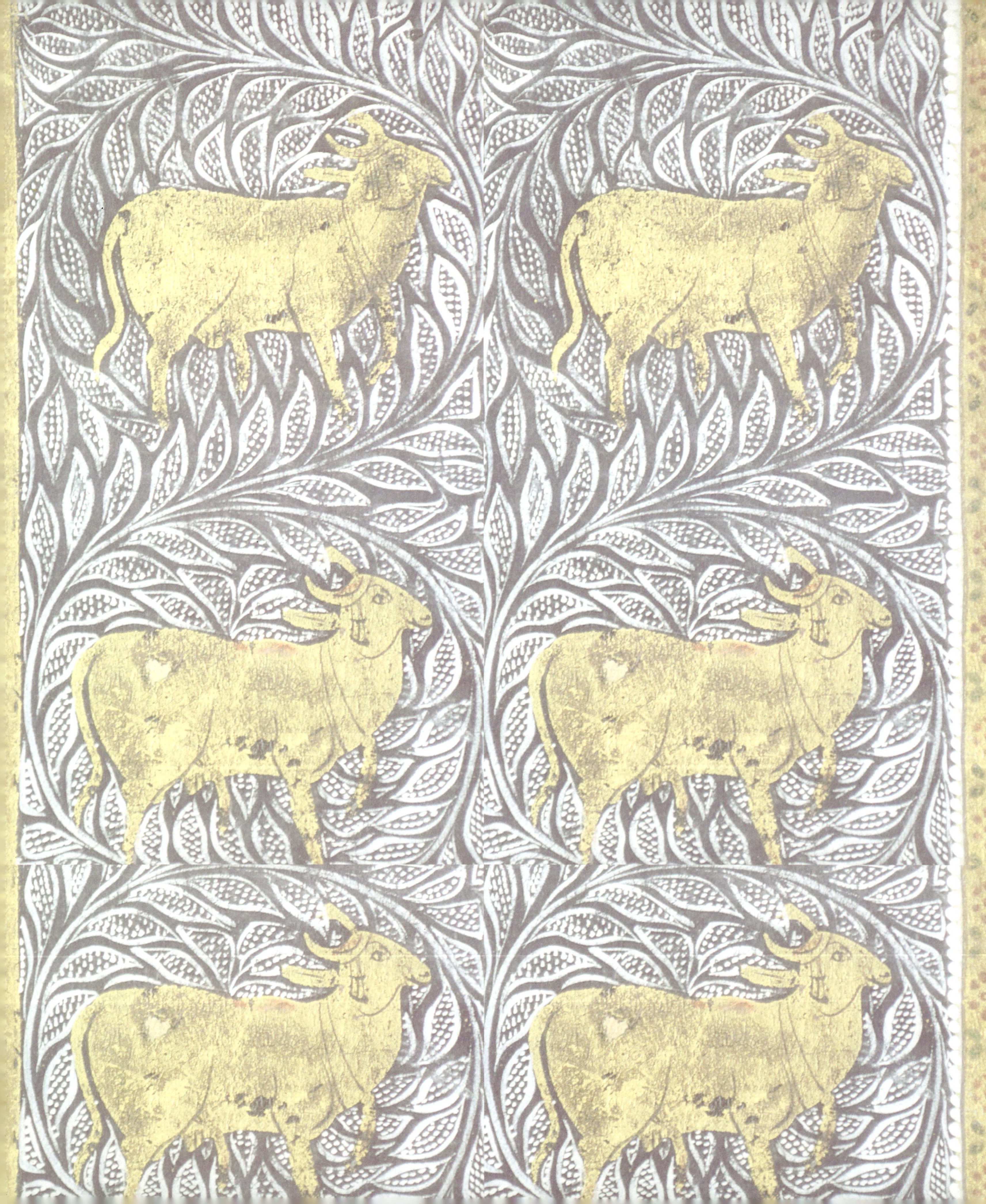